HEALTHY PESCATARIAN COOKBOOK

200 Easy Ingredients Recipes To Start Healthier Lifestyle With Pescatarian Diet Meal Preparation For Beginners Including Gluten-free Recipes and for Kids!

By

Nicole Rachel Walker

Table of Contents

Introduction

Over the past decade, people have been thinking a lot about the foods they consume. Not only are people concerned about the consumption of healthy foods to provide nutrients to the body, but they are also interested in consuming foods that are not full of preservatives or additives. People are looking for ways to eat less processed foods, which are more sustainable for the entire planet.

Recently, this trend has turned many people into vegetarians or even vegans, both options respected.

However, some people find that when they remove animal protein from their diets and are not able to eat healthily through a balanced fish diet, they are not able to get enough protein in their diets.

Instead of giving up all animal protein, many people change their diet, including fish. The reason for this is that the fish contains a lot of healthy protein, has low-fat content, and has good fats due to their stable source. In Alaska, for example, fishers help maintain the midi population by harvesting only major males that meet the minimum requirements.

This way, fishers can be sure that they are not harvesting fish that are still growing and that they are not harvesting female fish that help the mussel skin to stay healthy through reproduction. Therefore, consumers can eat raw males without having to affect the fish population in Alaska.

In recent books like The Omnivore Dilemma and movies like Food in Cup, they made people aware of how the food industry and food are actually consumed.

Unfortunately, although the fishing industry has paid much less attention to the meat industry, so many people do not know that. As long as they consume the main men instead of the female and baby middens, they can do so without harming the environment's healthy fishes.

Instead of becoming mostly vegetarians or full vegetarians, people can use a healthy diet to achieve the nutritional value they need without harming the environment, just like a diet, eat a meal full of beef, pork, or chicken.

Fish also has nutritional characteristics that are not known to exist in any other animal or plant-based foods. Many varieties of fish are uniquely high in both vitamin D and the essential omega-3 fatty acids known as docosahexaenoic acid (DHA) and eicosapentaenoic acid (EPA). No other naturally occurring foods in our food system are as individually rich in either of these essential nutrients, and no other foods contain both at such high levels.

No wonder omega-3 and vitamin D supplements have become so popular in recent years. According to current data from Nutrients and The Journal of Nutrition, many Americans struggle to get enough omega-3 fatty acids and vitamin D in their diets. Certain groups, such as vegans, understandably may not get an adequate amount of these nutrients from their diet alone. For the rest of us, the best way to prevent and reverse these nutritional shortcomings is to eat more fish.

Each of us develops our own unique nutritional lifestyle based on our personal situation and health or ethical or environmental concerns. Therefore, your specific dietary lifestyle will likely look different from mine. If you're going from eating meat to eliminating it (as opposed to starting as a vegetarian and adding fish into your diet), you may be letting go of eating habits you are accustomed to. It may feel different for a while to get used to cooking and ordering meals that contain no meat or poultry. In addition, you may be unfamiliar with some of the ingredients you'll be using once you start cooking primarily plant-based meals.

This fantastic guide talks about the Pescatarian diet and how you can make some of the finest delicacies.

Chapter 1. What Is the Pescatarian Diet

The term pescatarian derives from the combination of the words "pesce" and "vegetarian." "Pesce" comes from the Italian language, meaning fish. This diet is seen as part of the vegetarian spectrum because it contains a large amount of plant-based foods.

A pescatarian does not eat meat, but they do eat fish and seafood. People often choose a pescatarian diet for health reasons, environmental concerns, and ethical reasons. A pescatarian diet lowers the risk of having chronic medical problems, such as heart disease. Seafood generally has a lower amount of fat and cholesterol than most meats, which is beneficial to the health of your heart.

Fatty fish contain omega-3 fatty acids (DHA and EPA), which also promote a healthy heart. DHA and EPA are linked to a decrease in high blood pressure and decrease the risk of heart disease. They may also lessen symptoms of rheumatoid arthritis and can be preventative of heart attacks. Stricter diets such as the vegetarian and vegan diet increase your risk of having a vitamin or mineral deficiency, as well as having fewer options for protein sources.

Pescatarians can quickly source these much-needed vitamins and minerals by eating a wide variety of seafood, whole grains, and produce.

Fish contain many nutrients and minerals such as vitamin D, B2 (riboflavin), iron, zinc, iodine, magnesium, potassium, and more. Fish is also rich in calcium and phosphorus, which are beneficial for bone health. Zinc is especially present in oysters, while mussels are a great source for iron and selenium. Clams are also rich in selenium, as well as calcium.

There are many environmental concerns regarding meat-eating diets. Meat production creates greenhouse gases and harms the environment. There are higher amounts of carbon emissions, increased land use, and increase the use of resources. Livestock release a substantial amount of methane, a greenhouse gas much more potent than carbon dioxide.

The feed product that is used to fatten the livestock requires large amounts of fertilizer, fuel, pesticides, and water. This takes millions of acres of cropland as well as millions of pounds of pesticides and fertilizer. The manure of the livestock, as well as the processing of the livestock and transportation of animals, yields a great amount of pollution and waste.

Many of the ethical reasons that people choose to pursue a pescatarian diet have to do with environmental concerns, as well as the treatment of animals. Some people also disagree with poor labor conditions and pursue this diet for humanitarian reasons. Some of these reasons include: not wanting to partake in killing animals for food, disagreeing with inhumane factory practices, not wanting to support the poor labor conditions that workers experience, and disagreeing with the land and resource use for animal feed and production because it is unjust.

If you are seeking a well-rounded healthy diet, wanting to decrease your environmental footprint, or agree with any of the ethical reasons, a pescatarian diet may be the ideal route for you.

Chapter 2. The Health Benefits of a Pescatarian Lifestyle

The way you feed your body can have a significant impact on your overall health. If you stick to a pescatarian eating plan, you will get all the benefits of a plant-based diet with the additional protein and nutrients of seafood. Plus, you'll eliminate the risks associated with eating meat. Here's just a taste of the benefits you could experience.

- **Brain health:** We all want healthy brains. Studies suggest eating fish may support this. A 2016 study showed that eating at least three servings of fish per week while you're pregnant could benefit the brain of your offspring. Research also shows that eating fish can lower the risk of developing Alzheimer's disease.

- **Heart health:** Opting for a pescatarian diet can be a way to nourish your heart. Oily fish, such as mackerel and salmon, are rich in omega-3 fatty acids, which have been shown to reduce the risk of fatal heart attacks and congestive heart failure. And studies have shown that people who follow a plant-based diet are less likely to develop coronary heart disease.

- **Inflammation:** Inflammation is associated with several diseases, and many of the foods in a pescatarian diet star in an anti-inflammatory diet, especially fatty fish, which are rich in omega-3 fats.

- **Minimizing cancer risk:** According to the American Institute for Cancer Research, limiting your intake of red meats and processed meats can reduce your risk of developing certain cancers.

- **Weight loss:** As mentioned earlier, those who follow a pescatarian diet have the potential to maintain or lose weight because of the lower calories and higher nutrient density of the foods most frequently eaten in this lifestyle.

Improves Heart Health

Your heart will thank you for eating the pescatarian way! One of the best-studied health benefits of following the pescatarian diet is improved heart health for men and women. Pescatarian diets are rich in omega-3 fatty acids, antioxidants, and fiber, and low in saturated fat. As mentioned above, anti-inflammatory omega-3 fatty acids, coupled with a high intake of vegetables, fruit, and whole-grains contribute to the lower risk of heart disease. The American Heart Association recommends eating fish twice weekly to reduce your risk of many heart diseases, including coronary heart disease, congestive heart failure, stroke, sudden cardiac death, and more.

Simplifies Weight Management

Eating a plant-rich diet makes this effortless! Many studies have shown that individuals who follow a plant-forward diet, including vegans, vegetarians, and pescatarians, have lower body mass indexes (BMI) compared to their meat-eating counterparts. Why? Likely because pescatarians and vegetarians fill up on more plants, which are low in calories and fat and high in fiber.

Reduces Risk of Type 2 Diabetes

The pescatarian diet is anti-inflammatory, high in omega-3 fatty acids, and rich in fiber, which all contribute to reducing the risk of type 2 diabetes. In fact, in the Adventist Health Study-2 cohort, with more than 70,000 individuals, pescatarians had the greatest flavonoid (a type of antioxidant) intake, which could be why plant-heavy diets may reduce the risk of developing type 2 diabetes by half.

Even more, replacing meat consumption with fish and plant-based proteins proves beneficial for individuals at risk for diabetes. Studies demonstrate an association between red meat consumption and incidence of type 2 diabetes.

Lowers Mortality Rate

A major study found that compared to meat-eaters, pescatarians had significantly lower mortality rates. No wonder the pescatarian lifestyle is growing in popularity! In addition to a plant-powered diet, this may be because of the anti-inflammatory omega-3 fatty acids in fish and lower saturated fat intake from not eating meat and poultry.

Diminishes Dementia Risk

Eating fish, especially fatty fish rich in omega-3 fatty acids, may benefit your brain health, too. Specifically, consuming fish once weekly was associated with a 60 percent lower risk of Alzheimer's disease, according to a study published in the Archives of Neurology. This is likely due to boosting your omega-3 fatty acid intake, plus a pescatarian diet is rich in antioxidants and low in saturated fat, which may protect against cognitive decline.

Reduces Cancer Risk

Following a vegetarian diet — and, even more precisely, a pesco-vegetarian diet — has been shown to reduce the risk of colorectal cancer (cancers of the colon and rectum). As a leading cause of cancer mortality, it may be especially important for individuals who are at increased risk for colon cancer to follow a pescatarian diet, including men and women over the age of 50, smokers, those with a family history of colon cancer, and individuals of African American or Hispanic descent.

Stocking Your Pescatarian Kitchen
- **Plant-Based Proteins**

By now, we've established that a pescatarian diet is more about eating mostly plants than it is about eating fish. In addition to the plant-based proteins listed, here are some additional staples to consider:

a. **Chia:** Consider making chia seeds a pantry staple so you can add a protein boost to smoothies and cereals and treat yourself to overnight chia pudding. Look for chia in the rice aisle, baking aisle, or health food aisle at the grocery store.

b. **Lentils:** These come in many varieties, from soft red lentils that cook up into a luscious soup to firm green French lentils du Puy.

c. **Oatmeal:** Oats are indeed a good protein source. I prefer the texture of steel-cut oats over rolled oats, even though they take longer to cook (look for 5-minute steel-cut oats if you're short on time).

d. **Pumpkin seeds (pepitas):** Look for pepitas (hulled pumpkin seeds), another complete protein, in the bulk section of the grocery store. Whether raw or roasted, plain or salted, they add a satisfying texture to salads and make a fine snack on their own.

- **Fish and Seafood**
  a. **Cod:** Labeled as true cod or Pacific cod, this fish is different from lingcod and sablefish (a.k.a. black cod). Look for flesh that is fairly translucent and not too opaque. Substitutes include black cod/ lingcod, grouper, halibut, sea bass, and snapper.
  b. **Mussels and clams:** As you want these to be alive until you cook them, look for tightly closed shells — if a shell opens a little, give it a tap to see if it closes (a sign of life). Also, make sure they smell fresh and like the sea — they shouldn't have a strong odor. Discard any dead or broken ones before cooking, or any that do not open after cooking.
  c. **Salmon:** Look for wild-caught salmon (the skin is a darker pink and the flesh is almost red) that appears moist (an indicator of freshness). And don't overlook canned salmon — canned pink or red salmon can be an excellent base for a salad when mixed with a little mayonnaise and a spoonful of drained capers.
  d. **Shrimp and prawns:** Despite their similarities, shrimp and prawns differ in their gills and number of clawed legs. Otherwise, they can often be used interchangeably as long as the size is consistent for the recipe. They are sold cooked or raw, frozen or thawed, shelled and deveined, or shell on (and perhaps head-on.)

- **Fresh or Frozen?**

  Although words like "fresh," "seasonal," "local," and "organic" seem to convey the best —the cream of the crop, if you will — there's no shame in frozen foods. I'm not talking about those preservative-laden frozen meals (that's another story). Rather, there are often benefits in choosing frozen ingredients over their fresh counterparts. Many types of fish are flash-frozen shortly after being caught, which means that by the time the fish reaches you, the consumer, it might be fresher than the "fresh" fish that's been refrigerated instead of frozen on route to you. Plus, frozen fish may be more convenient if you live in an area without easy access to fresh fish. Pay special attention to the labels — look for information about where the fish is caught and whether it's wild or farmed, especially in the case of shrimp, which can be hard to find wild and domestic

- **Fruits and Vegetables**

  One of my favorite things to do when I need some culinary inspiration is to head to the produce aisle and see what I can find. Sometimes trying something new or unusual is a great way to get the creative juices flowing. And when it comes to "eating the rainbow," this is an excellent place to begin.

  a. **Avocado:** Full of healthy fats, and with its satisfying creaminess, avocado is great for everything from topping salads or toast to blending into a smoothie.

  b. **Potatoes:** Russet, Yukon Gold, red new potatoes, fingerling potatoes — there's plenty of variety here to keep things interesting.

  c. **Mushrooms:** Since some types of mushrooms are a great source of vitamin B12, these are a valuable ingredient in a plant-based diet. Sautéed or grilled, they're easy to cook and lend a pleasant, sometimes meaty, texture to your plate.

  d. **Broccoli and cauliflower:** These are delicious served raw — with hummus or a creamy dip — or simply roasted with olive oil and salt and are worth keeping in the refrigerator at all times.

  e. **Onion:** A bag of onions lasts a long time if stored properly, so go ahead and stock up. Chopped white and yellow onions will get many recipes started. When added raw after plating, thinly sliced red onion provides flavor and color to many dishes.

f. **Greens (kale, spinach, chard, romaine):** These are so good for you. Served raw in salads, braised or sautéed, or steamed, they're versatile too.

g. **Zucchini:** About as versatile as can be, when sliced lengthwise and roasted with olive oil and salt, zucchini makes a simple yet satisfying side. Or, spiralized into long strands and cooked briefly in salted water makes zucchini a stand-in for pasta.

h. **Tomatoes:** One of the pleasures of the summer months, tomatoes are full of flavor when they're in season — a drizzle of your best olive oil and a scattering of flaky salt is all you need to make a fresh side. Any time of year, however, bite-size grape or cherry tomatoes can be juicy additions to salads, and slow-roasting or simmering with other seasonings can bring out their flavor.

i. **Bell pepper:** Sliced, these are one of the best ways to scoop up a flavorful dip! Diced, they're a crunchy and healthy addition to salads.

j. **Carrots:** Whether shredded and dressed in oil, spices, and herbs to make a salad or chopped and added to a soup, keeping a bag of carrots in the refrigerator will serve you well.

Chapter 3. Important Kitchen Instruments

Must-Have

- **Good quality knives:** Some good, sharp knives make all the difference when cooking at home. The knife that is most needed is the chef's knife, necessary for cutting vegetables, fresh herbs, and other ingredients. Also useful is a serrated knife for cutting and slicing tomatoes, melons, citrus fruits and peppers, and a paring knife.

- **A set of stainless-steel mixing bowls (small, medium, and large):** A basic set of mixing bowls is essential in any kitchen. Stainless steel is lightweight and durable and the bowls can be attached for storage. However, keep in mind that stainless steel generates heat and should not be used in the microwave.

- **A set of pots and pans (small, medium, large, and extremely large):** Cisterns are basic tools for anglers. Sautéing is one of the most effective and tasty ways to prepare healthy dishes, especially those that contain fish. The utensils and pots are available in various sizes. Medium pots are ideal for cooked puddings and pasta sauces. Large and very large pots are required for soups, stews, and pasta cooking.

- **Food processor or blender:** A food processor is an extremely versatile tool. You can use it to cut or chop vegetables, puree soups, and combine dry ingredients, among other uses. A blender works just as well and is a great way to make smoothies.

- **Chopping boards:** Food safety experts recommend the use of different cutters for meat and vegetables. Both plastic and wooden cutting boards are safe to use, although plastic may be better for your fish. Note that plastic cutting boards are more comfortable to sanitize, but need to be changed more frequently.

As the name implies, you can live without beautiful objects. But they will definitely add more flexibility and variety to the types of dishes you can prepare and how you can prepare them.

- **Spiralizer:** The spiralizer is a kitchen tool that cuts vegetables into long threads that look like thin spaghetti. It gives you some fun cooking options and lets you make more with veggies like zucchini and sweet potatoes. You can use these vegetable "noodles" as a substitute for low-carb pasta or add texture to salads.

- **An assortment of baking dishes:** Glass and ceramic baking dishes come in a variety of shapes and sizes. Whether they are square, rectangular, or oval, baking dishes are great for cooking casseroles, roasting fish or vegetables, or baking breakfast treats and desserts.

- **Thermometer:** You can often tell when fish is fully cooked by looking to see if the flesh is opaque and by checking that it flakes easily when tested with a fork. An instant-read meat thermometer can be a helpful tool if you prefer to be more exact (the FDA recommends that most seafood be cooked to an internal temperature of 145°F).

What a Pescatarian Eats

Pesce means "fish" in Italian, so it's easy enough to conclude that a pescatarian is a vegetarian who eats fish. But is it that simple? Well, sort of. Just to make sure we're clear and not missing any of the incredible food groups available in the pescatarian lifestyle, here's an overview of the foods pescatarians eat.

- **Beans, lentils, and legumes:** This category also includes soy products like edamame, tofu, and tempeh. And don't forget chickpeas, which make delectable hummus.

- **Eggs:** Pescatarians differ on eggs — some choose to eat them, some omit them. It's up to you.

- **Dairy products:** As with eggs, some pescatarians eat milk, cheese, yogurt, kefir, and other dairy products, whereas others avoid these foods.

- **Fruits:** When eaten at the peak of ripeness, fruit can be as satisfying as a sugar-laden dessert.

- **Nuts and seeds:** These can be used in a medley of ways to add an abundance of interesting and intriguing flavors and textures to your meals and snacks.

- **Seafood:** Any type of fish or seafood that comes from a river, lake, bay, or ocean is fair game for a pescatarian.

- **Vegetables:** There's no chance of boredom with the wide range of colors, textures, and flavors available from vegetables!

- **Whole grains:** When paired with other plant-based foods, whole grains like barley, rice, oats, and bread can help create complete proteins, which are important for people following a mostly plant-based diet.

What a Pescatarian Doesn't Eat

Though it may go without saying, here's a look at what you'll be leaving off the grocery list when you convert to a pescatarian lifestyle:

- **Organ meat**. Avoid all organ meats and offal — including liver, tongue, sweetbreads, tripe, and chitterlings.

- **Red meat.** Pescatarians avoid all meats that come from mammals and are red in their raw state (beef, lamb, pork, veal, venison).

- **Wild game**. Although less popular than red meat and white meat, game meats — including pheasant, rabbit, venison, and wild boar — won't make an appearance on a pescatarian's plate.

- **White meat**. Poultry, such as chicken, duck, goose, and turkey, are also off-limits.

Chapter 4. BREAKFAST

1. EASY, HEALTHY GREEK SALMON SALAD

Easy / Gluten-free

Preparation time: 10 minutes

Cooking time: 8 minutes

Servings: 4

Ingredients:

- ¼ cup olive oil
- 3 tablespoons red wine vinegar
- 2 tablespoons freshly crush lemon juice (from 1 lemon)
- 1 clove of garlic, chopped
- ¾ teaspoon dried oregano
- 1/2 teaspoon Kosher salt
- ¼ teaspoon fresh black pepper
- 1 finely chopped red onion
- A cup of cold water
- 4 (6 oz.) salmon fillets, peeled
- 2 medium-sized Korean salads, such as Boston or Bibb (about 1 kilogram), broken into bite-size pieces
- 2 medium-sized tomatoes, cut into 1-inch pieces
- 1 medium English cucumber, quadrilateral and then cut into 1/2-inch pieces
- ½ cup of half-length Kalamata olives
- 4 oz. Feta Cheese, minced (about 1 cup)

Directions:

1. In the middle of the oven arrange a shelf and heat to 425 degrees Fahrenheit. While the oven is warming, marinate the salmon and soften the onion (instructions below).

2. Put the olive oil, vinegar, lemon juice, garlic, oregano, salt, and pepper in a large bowl, then transfer three tablespoons of vinegar large enough into a baking dish to keep all the salmon chunks in one layer. Add the salmon, lightly rotate a few times to wrap evenly in the wings. Cover the fridge. Pour the onion and water into a small bowl and set aside 10 minutes to make the onion stronger. Drain and release the liquid.

3. Discover the salmon and grill for 8 to 12 minutes until they are cooked and lightly fried. The thermometer instant-read in the middle of the thickest tab should record 120 degrees Fahrenheit to 130 degrees Fahrenheit for the rare medium or 135 degrees Fahrenheit to 145 degrees Fahrenheit. The total

time of the cooking depends on the thickness of the salmon, depending on the thickest portion of the fillet. It Al depends on the salad.

4. Add the salad, tomatoes, cucumbers, olives, and red onion to the Gina Vine bowl and salt to combine. Divide into four plates or shallow bowl. When the salmon is ready, place one fillet over each salad. Sprinkle with feta and serve quickly.

Nutrition:

- **Calories:** 351;
- **Total fat:** 4 g;
- **Cholesterol:** 94 mg;
- **Fiber:** 2 g;
- **Protein:** 12 g;
- **Sodium:** 327 mg

2. <u>MEDITERRANEAN PEPPER</u>

Easy/Gluten-free/Dairy-free

Preparation time: 5 minutes

Cooking time: 20 minutes

Servings: 4

Ingredients:

- 1 tablespoon
- 1 can be clear out
- 1/2 teaspoon restrained oil 1/2 cup sun-dried tomatoes
- 2 cups of spinach (fresh or frozen)

- 1/2 spoon drops of zaatar spices
- 10 eggs, screaming
- 1/2 cup Feta cheese
- 1-2 tablespoons
- Destroy salt and pepper

Directions:

1. At 350 degrees Fahrenheit, firstly preheat the oven

2. Heat a cast-iron boiler over medium heat. Add the olive oil and peas, slowly and slowly cooking until you want to release the liquid and start to brown and brown. Then, sauté the sun-dried tomatoes with a little reserved oil, spinach, and zucchini, and cook for 2-3 minutes until the spinach is crushed.

3. When the spinach has faded, pour the vegetable mixture evenly into the cast iron fish and then add the boiled eggs, turning the pan so that the eggs cover the vegetables evenly. Bake on medium heat until the eggs start about halfway through. Pour the eggs and vegetables with the spatula into the pan, leave the eggs to cook until the frittata is placed.

4. When the eggs are almost half cooked, add the Feta cheese and spoon the horseradish sauce on top and dust with salt and pepper. Remove the cast iron from the oven and place it in the middle rack in the oven. Bake until cooked on the ferrite, will take about five minutes.

5. Bring out from the oven and let it cool slightly. For cedar, cut or square the pie and pour with a pan.

Nutrition:

- **Calories:** 311;
- **Total fat:** 4 g;
- **Cholesterol:** 84 mg;
- **Fiber**: 2 g;
- **Protein:** 12 g;
- **Sodium:** 357 mg

3. BLACK BEANS AND SWEET POTATO TACOS

Medium/Dairy-free

Preparation time: 10 minutes

Cooking time: 30 minutes

Servings: 6

Ingredients:

- 1 lb. sweet potato (about 2 medium teaspoons), skin cut and cut into 1/2-inch pieces

- Divide into 2 tablespoons of olive oil
- 1 tablespoon Kosher salt, divided
- ¼ teaspoon fresh black pepper on large white or yellow onion, finely chopped
- 2 teaspoons of red pepper
- 1 cumin with a teaspoon
- 1 (15 oz.) can be black beans, drained and drained
- Cup of water
- ¼ cup freshly chopped garlic
- 12 pcs. Corn
- To serve: Guacamole
- Sliced cheese or feta cheese (optional)
- Wood Wedge

Directions:

1. In the oven, set out a shelf in the middle and place to 425 degrees Fahrenheit. Set a big sheet of aluminum foil on the work surface. Collect the tortillas from the top and wrap them completely in foil. Put it aside

2. Put sweet potatoes on a small baking sheet. Mix with one tablespoon oil and sprinkle with 1/2 teaspoon salt and 1/4 teaspoon black pepper. Discard to mix and play in one layer. Fry for 20 minutes. Sprinkle the potatoes with a flat lid and set aside until a corner of the oven is clear.

3. Put the foil wrapping in the empty space and continue to cook for about 10 minutes until the sweet potatoes are browned and stained and the seasonings are heated. Also, cook the beans.

4. You then heat one tablespoon remaining in a large skillet over low heat. Put the onion and cook, occasionally stirring, until translucent, about 3 minutes. Mix the pepper powder, cumin, and 1/2 teaspoon salt. Add the beans and water.

5. Shield the pan and reduce the heat to low heat. Cook for 5 minutes, then slice and use the back of the fork to chop the beans a little, about half of the total. If there is still water in the vessel, stir the exposed mixture for about 30 seconds until evaporated.

6. Peel the sweet potatoes and add the cantaloupe to the black beans and mix. If used, fill the yolk with a mixture of black beans and top with guacamole and cheese. Serve with lime wedges.

Nutrition:

- **Calories:** 251;
- **Total fat:** 4 g;
- **Cholesterol:** 94 mg;

- **Fiber:** 2 g;
- **Protein:** 15 g;
- **Sodium:** 329 mg

4. <u>**SEAFOOD COOKED FROM BEER**</u>

Medium/Gluten-free/Dairy-free

Preparation time: 30 minutes

Cooking time: 1 hour

Servings: 8

Ingredients:

SEAFOOD:

- Canola oil for roasting
- 1/2 Cup Coarse cornmeal
- 1/2 tablespoon red pepper
- 1/4 baking soda
- 1 1/2 Cup Flour for all purposes is divided
- Kosher salt and freshly ground black pepper
- 1 12 oz. can drink beer in style
- 1 code and skin without skin, cut into 8 strips
- 1 large cup (number 25/25) of peeled and spread shrimp (remaining tail)
- 16 percentiles, shake
- 1 lemon sliced with cedar wedge
- Tartar sauce, mignon, chimichurri, hot sauce, and malt vinegar, for cedar

FOR TARTAR SAUCE:

- 1/2 cup Mayonnaise
- 2 teaspoons, pickled, chopped or pureed
- 1 tablespoon fresh lemon juice
- 1 tablespoon three-quarter pants
- 1 tablespoon mustard
- Kosher salt and freshly ground black pepper

INGREDIENTS:

- 1/2 cup red wine vinegar
- 1 small rest, finely chopped
- Kosher salt and freshly ground black pepper

CHIMICHURRI:

- 1/2 Cup Fresh parsley on a flat-leaf
- 1/4 cup White wine vinegar
- 2 tablespoons olive oil
- 2 cloves of minced garlic
- 1 stem, seeds, and mincemeat
- 1 tablespoon fresh oregano, chopped
- Kosher salt

Directions:

1. Heat 1 1/2-inch oil in a large Dutch oven over medium heat at 375 degrees F (deep-fried temperature with a thermometer).

2. Meanwhile, chop corn, bell pepper, baking soda, 1 cup of flour, 1/2 teaspoon salt, and 1/2 teaspoon pepper in a bowl. Add the broth and the phloem to mix.

3. Put 1/2 cup of the remaining flour in a bowl. Add salt, pepper, and the fish, shrimps, shells, and lemon slices and serve little.

4. Work several pieces at once, remove the seafood and the lemons from the flour, shake too much, and drain the dough and allow the excess drops to return to the container. Carefully add the hot oil, being careful not to overload the pot. Roast golden brown and cook for 1 to 2 minutes. Transfer to a sheet of paper towel — season with salt.

5. **Make the tartar sauce:** mayonnaise, pickled or mixed the cloves, and pour the lemon juice, pepper, and mustard whole in a bowl. Season with Kosher salt and freshly ground pepper, feel free to add more lemon juice. Face 2/3 glass.

6. **To make mignonette:** add red wine vinegar and finely minced mustard in a bowl. Season with Kosher salt and freshly ground pepper allow standing for at least 30 minutes or up to 24 hours. Make 1/2 cup.

7. **Make chimichurri:** Combine parsley, white wine vinegar, olive oil, garlic, jalapeño, and fresh oregano in a bowl. It is seasoned with Kosher salt. Face 2/3 glass.

8. It is served with lemon wedges, tartar sauce, mignon, chimiches, hot sauce, and malt vinegar.

Nutrition:

- **Calories:** 221;
- **Total fat:** 4 g;
- **Cholesterol:** 94 mg;
- **Fiber:** 2 g;
- **Protein:** 12 g;

5. <u>CRAB CHICKEN</u>

Medium/Dairy-free

Preparation time: 20 minutes

Cooking time: 40 minutes

Servings: 8

Ingredients:

- Canola oil for roasting
- 1c coarse corn flour
- 1/2 Cup Flour, spoon, and surface used
- 3/4 Cup Baking powder
- 1/2 spoon
- 1/4 tablespoon
- Kosher salt
- 2 arpagic, finely chopped
- 1 tablespoon crushed peas
- Eat 8 ounces of claw crab meat (2.11 c)
- 4 oz. of Gruyère cheese, chilled (about 1 cup)
- 1 c Dough water
- 1 you tie

Directions:

1. Heat 1 1/2-inch oil in a large Dutch oven over medium heat up to 350 degrees F (deep-fry).

2. Meanwhile, mix the cornmeal, flour, baking powder, cayenne, baking soda, and 3/4 teaspoon salt in a bowl. Add onion and onion and mix to combine. Add the crab meat and cheese and mix with a fork to combine. In the center of a well, add the butter and egg and mix to combine.

3. Spoon soup into the hot oil and be careful not to spill the pan and fry, occasionally turning until browned, 3 to 5 minutes. Transfer to a sheet of paper towel — season with salt repeat with the remaining dough.

Nutrition:

- **Calories:** 351;
- **Total fat:** 4 g;
- **Cholesterol:** 94 mg;
- **Fiber:** 2 g;

- **Protein:** 12 g;
- **Sodium:** 319 mg

6. <u>SLOW LENTIL SOUP</u>

Easy/Gluten-free

Preparation time: 10 minutes

Cooking time: 20 minutes

Servings: 6

Ingredients:

- 4 cups (1 quart) of low sodium vegetable juice
- 1 (14 oz.) tomatoes can (no leak)
- 1 small, fried yellow onion
- 1 medium carrot, sliced
- 1 medium-sized celery stalk, one-piece
- 1 cup green lentils
- 1 teaspoon of olive oil, plus more for cedar
- 2 cloves of garlic, turn
- 1 teaspoon Kosher salt
- 1 teaspoon tomato paste
- 1 leaf
- 1/2 teaspoon below ground
- 1/2 teaspoon of ground coriander
- 1/4 teaspoon of smoked peppers
- 2 tablespoons red wine vinegar
- Serving options: plain yogurt, olive oil, freshly chopped parsley or coriander leaves

Directions:

1. Put all ingredients, except vinegar, in a slow cooker for 1/3 to 2-4 quarts and mix to combine. Cover and cook in the low settings for about 8 hours until the lentil is tender.

2. Remove bay leaf and mix in red wine vinegar. If desired, place a pot, a drop of olive oil, and fresh parsley or crushed liquid in a bowl.

Nutrition:

- **Calories:** 231;
- **Total fat:** 4 g;
- **Cholesterol:** 64 mg;

- **Fiber:** 2 g;
- **Protein:** 12 g;
- **Sodium:** 368 mg

7. LIGHT BANG SHRIMP PASTE

Medium/Dairy-free

Preparation time: 10 minutes

Cooking time: 20 minutes

Servings: 4

Ingredients:

FOR CRUNCHY CRUMBS:

- 1 tablespoon oil without butter
- Fresh cups or pancakes
- 1/8 teaspoon Kosher salt
- 1/8 teaspoon fresh black pepper
- Pepper racks
- Spend garlic powder

FOR SHRIMP PASTA:

- Cooking spray
- ½ cup of Greek yogurt whole milk
- 2 tablespoons of Asian sweet pepper sauce, such as the iconic eel
- 1 teaspoon of honey
- ¼ teaspoon of garlic powder
- The juice is divided into 2 medium lemons (about 1/4 glass)
- 12 ounces of dried spaghetti
- 1 cup shrimp without skin and peeled
- 1 teaspoon Kosher salt, plus for pasta juice
- ¼ teaspoon fresh black pepper
- 1/8 teaspoon cayenne pepper
- 2 moderated onions, sliced, sliced

Directions:

Make crisp crumbs:

Over low heat, defrost the butter in a skillet. Add crumbs, salt, black pepper, cayenne pepper, and garlic powder.

Cook while constantly stirring, until golden, crispy, and fragrant. It will take 4 - 5 minutes, then put it aside.

<u>Make shrimps:</u>

1. Place a shelf in the middle of the oven and heat to 400 degrees Fahrenheit. Cover with a lightly cooked baking sheet with cooking spray. Put it aside

2. Boil salt water in a big pot. Meanwhile, chop yogurt, pepper sauce, honey, garlic powder, and half of the lemon juice in a small bowl. Put it aside

3. Put the pasta when the water is boiling and boil the pasta for up to 10 minutes or as instructed. Dry the shrimps and place them on a sheet of ready-made cooking. Season with salt, black pepper, and coffee and mix to cook. It stretches in a uniform layer. Roast once, until the shrimps are matte and pink, 6 to 8 minutes. Pour the remaining lemon juice over the shrimps and pour over it and pour the flavored pieces onto the baking sheet.

4. Evacuate the pasta and return it to the pot. Pour into the yogurt sauce and serve until well cooked. Put shrimp and juice on the baking sheet with half of the onion and lightly add it again. Generously sprinkle each portion with a crunchy crumb and remaining onion. Serve immediately.

Nutrition:

- **Calories:** 351;
- **Total fat:** 4 g;
- **Cholesterol:** 94 mg;
- **Fiber:** 2 g;
- **Protein:** 12 g;
- **Sodium:** 327 mg

8. SWEET AND SMOKED SALMON

Easy/Dairy-free

Preparation time: 35 minutes

Cooking time: 1 hour

Servings: 8

Ingredients:

- 2 tablespoons light brown sugar
- 2 tablespoons smoked peppers
- 1 tablespoon shaved lemon peel
- Kosher salt
- Freshly chopped black pepper
- Salmon fillets on the skin 1/2 kilogram

Directions:

1. Soak a large plate (about 15 cm by 7 inches) in water for 1 to 2 hours.

2. It is heated over medium heat. Combine sugar, pepper, lemon zest, and 1/2 teaspoon of salt and pepper in a bowl. Mix the salmon with the salt and rub the mixture of spices in all parts of the meat.

3. Put the salmon on the wet plate, skin down — oven, covered, in the desired color, 25 to 28 minutes for medium.

Nutrition:

- **Calories:** 321;
- **Total fat:** 4 g;
- **Cholesterol:** 54 mg;
- **Protein:** 12 g;
- **Sodium:** 337 mg

9. CHOCOLATE CHERRY CRUNCH GRANOLA

Easy/Dairy-free

Preparation time: 10 minutes

Cooking time: 20 minutes

Servings: 6

Ingredients:

- 3 cups rolled oats
- 2 cups assorted seeds, such as sesame, chia, sunflower, and pepitas (hulled pumpkin seeds)
- 1 cup sliced almonds
- 1 cup unsweetened coconut flakes
- 2 teaspoons vanilla extract
- 2 teaspoons ground cinnamon
- 1 teaspoon fine sea salt
- ½ cup of cocoa powder
- ½ cup pure maple syrup
- ¼ cup coconut oil or canola oil
- 1 cup dried cherries (unsweetened, if possible)
- 1 cup of chocolate chips

Directions:

1. Preheat the oven to 350°F. Spread 2 large baking sheets with parchment paper.
2. In a large bowl, stir together the oats, seeds, almonds, and coconut. Add the vanilla, cinnamon, salt, and cocoa powder. Stir to combine.
3. In a frypan over low heat, heat the maple syrup and coconut oil. Pour the warm syrup and oil over the oat mixture and stir to coat. On the prepared baking sheets, spread the granola in even layers.
4. Bake for 15 to 18 minutes, scraping and mixing occasionally, then remove from the oven.
5. Put in the dried cherries and chocolate chips, then return to the oven, now turned off but still warm, and let the granola cool and dry completely.

Nutrition:

- **Calories:** 570;
- **Total fat:** 31 g;
- **Cholesterol:** 94 mg;
- **Fiber:** 2 g;
- **Protein:** 12 g;

- **Sodium:** 204 mg

10. CREAMY RASPBERRY POMEGRANATE SMOOTHIE

Medium/Gluten-free

Preparation time: 5 minutes

Cooking time: 5 minutes

Servings: 1

Ingredients:

- 1½ cup pomegranate juice
- ½ cup unsweetened coconut milk
- 1 scoop vanilla protein powder (plant-based if you need it to be dairy-free)
- 2 packed cups fresh baby spinach
- 1 cup frozen raspberries
- 1 frozen banana (see Tip)
- 1 to 2 tablespoons freshly compressed lemon juice

Directions:

1. In a blender, combine the pomegranate juice and coconut milk. Add the protein powder and spinach. Give these a whirl to break down the spinach.

2. Add the raspberries, banana, and lemon juice, then top it off with ice. Blend until smooth and frothy.

Nutrition:

- **Calories:** 303;
- **Total fat:** 3 g;
- **Cholesterol:** 0 mg;
- **Fiber:** 2 g;
- **Protein:** 15 g;
- **Sodium:** 165 mg

11. MANGO COCONUT OATMEAL

Easy/Dairy-free

Preparation time: 5 minutes

Cooking time: 5 minutes

Servings: 2

Ingredients:

- 1½ cups water
- ½ cup 5-minute steel cut oats

- ¼ cup unsweetened canned coconut milk, plus more for serving (optional)
- 1 tablespoon pure maple syrup
- ⅛ teaspoon kosher salt
- 1 teaspoon sesame seeds
- Dash ground cinnamon
- 1 mango, stripped, pitted, and divide into slices
- 1 tablespoon unsweetened coconut flakes

Direction:

1. In a small frypan over high heat, boil water. Put the oats and lower the heat. Cook, stirring occasionally, for 5 minutes.
2. Put in the coconut milk, maple syrup, and salt to combine.
3. Get two bowls and sprinkle with the sesame seeds and cinnamon. Top with sliced mango and coconut flakes.

Nutrition:

- **Calories:** 373;
- **Total fat:** 11 g;
- **Cholesterol:** 0 mg;
- **Fiber:** 2 g;
- **Protein:** 12 g;
- **Sodium:** 167 mg

12. SPICED SWEET POTATO HASH WITH CILANTRO-LIME CREAM

Easy/Gluten-free

Preparation time: 20 minutes

Cooking time: 30 minutes

Servings: 2

Ingredients:

FOR THE CILANTRO-LIME CREAM:

- 1 avocado, halved and pitted
- ¼ cup packed fresh cilantro leaves and stems
- 2 tablespoons freshly squeezed lime juice
- 1 garlic clove, peeled
- 1 teaspoon kosher salt
- ½ teaspoon ground cumin

- 2 tablespoons extra-virgin olive oil

FOR THE HASH:

- ½ teaspoon kosher salt
- 1 large sweet potato, peeled and cut into ¾-inch pieces
- 2 tablespoons extra-virgin olive oil
- 1 onion, thinly sliced
- 2 garlic cloves, crushed
- 1 red bell pepper, thinly sliced
- 1 teaspoon ground cumin
- ¼ teaspoon ground turmeric
- Pinch freshly ground black pepper
- 2 tablespoons fresh cilantro leaves, chopped
- ½ jalapeño pepper, seeded and chopped (optional)
- Hot sauce, for serving (optional)

Directions:

To make the cilantro-lime cream:

Add the avocado flesh in a food compressor. Add the cilantro, lime juice, garlic, salt, and cumin. Whirl until smooth. When the processor is running slowly, softly. Taste and adjust seasonings, as needed. If you don't have a food processor or blender, simply mash the avocado well with a fork; the results will have more texture, but will still work. Cover and refrigerate until ready to serve.

To make the hash:

1. Boil salt-water in a medium pot over high heat. Add the sweet potato and cook for about 20 minutes until tender. Drain thoroughly.

2. Heat olive oil in a big skillet over low heat until it shimmers. Add the onion and sauté for about 4 minutes until translucent. Put the garlic and cook, turning, for about 30 seconds. Add the cooked sweet potato and red bell pepper. Season the hash with cumin, salt, turmeric, and pepper. For 5 to 7 minutes, sauté until the sweet potatoes are golden and the red bell pepper is soft.

3. Divide the sweet potatoes between 2 bowls and spoon the sauce over them. Scatter the cilantro and jalapeño (if using) over each and serve with hot sauce (if using).

Nutrition:

- **Calories:** 520;
- **Total fat:** 43 g;
- **Cholesterol:** 0 mg;

- **Fiber:** 2 g;
- **Protein:** 12 g;
- **Sodium:** 1719 mg

13. OPEN-FACE EGG SANDWICHES WITH CILANTRO-JALAPEÑO SPREAD

Easy/Dairy-free

Preparation time: 20 minutes

Cooking time: 10 minutes

Servings: 2

Ingredients:

FOR THE CILANTRO AND JALAPEÑO SPREAD:

- 1 cup filled up fresh cilantro leaves and stems (about 1 bunch)
- 1 jalapeño pepper, seeded and roughly chopped
- ½ cup extra-virgin olive oil
- ¼ cup pepitas (hulled pumpkin seeds), raw or roasted
- 2 garlic cloves, thinly sliced
- 1 tablespoon freshly squeezed lime juice
- 1 teaspoon kosher salt

FOR THE EGGS:

- 4 large eggs
- ¼ cup milk
- ¼ to ½ teaspoon kosher salt
- 2 tablespoons butter

FOR THE SANDWICH:

- 2 slices bread
- 1 tablespoon butter
- 1 avocado, halved, pitted, and divided into slices
- Microgreens or sprouts, for garnish

Directions:

To make the cilantro and jalapeño spread:

In a food processor, combine the cilantro, jalapeño, oil, pepitas, garlic, lime juice, and salt. Whirl until smooth. Refrigerate if making in advance; otherwise set aside.

To make the eggs:

1. In a medium bowl, whisk the eggs, milk, and salt.

2. Dissolve the butter in a skillet over low heat, swirling to coat the bottom of the pan. Pour in the whisked eggs. Cook until they start to set on the bottom, then, using a heatproof spatula, push them to the sides, allowing the uncooked portions to run into the bottom of the skillet. Continue until the eggs are set.

To assemble the sandwiches:

1. Toast the bed and spread with butter.

2. Spread a spoonful of the cilantro-jalapeño spread on each piece of toast. Top each with scrambled eggs.

3. Arrange avocado over each sandwich and garnish with microgreens.

Nutrition:

- **Calories:** 711;
- **Total fat:** 4 g;
- **Cholesterol:** 54 mg;
- **Fiber:** 12 g;
- **Protein:** 12 g;
- **Sodium:** 327 mg

14. SCRAMBLED EGGS WITH SOY SAUCE AND BROCCOLI SLAW

Medium/Gluten-free

Preparation time: 5 minutes

Cooking time: 10 minutes

Servings: 2

Ingredients:

- 1 tablespoon peanut oil, divided

- 4 large eggs
- ½ to 1 tablespoon soy sauce, tamari, or Bragg's liquid aminos
- 1 tablespoon water
- 1 cup shredded broccoli slaw or other shredded vegetables
- Kosher salt
- Chopped fresh cilantro, for serving
- Hot sauce, for serving

Directions:

1. In a medium nonstick skillet or cast-iron skillet over medium heat, heat 2 teaspoons of peanut oil, swirling to coat the skillet.

2. In a small bowl, whip the eggs, soy sauce, and water until smooth. Pour the eggs into the pan and let the bottom set. Using a wooden spoon, spread the eggs from one side to the other a couple of times so the uncooked portions on top pool into the bottom. Cook until the eggs are set.

3. In a medium container, stir together the broccoli slaw, remaining 1 teaspoon of peanut oil, and a touch of salt. Divide the slaw between 2 plates.

4. Top with the eggs and scatter cilantro on each serving. Serve with hot sauce.

Nutrition:
- **Calories:** 222;
- **Total fat:** 4 g;
- **Cholesterol:** 374 mg;
- **Fiber:** 2 g;
- **Protein:** 12 g;
- **Sodium**: 737 mg

15. <u>TASTE OF NORMANDY SALAD</u>

Easy/Gluten-free/Vegan

Preparation time: 25 minutes

Cook Time: 5 minutes

Servings: 4 to 6

Ingredients:

FOR THE WALNUTS:

- 2 tablespoons butter
- ¼ cup sugar or honey
- 1 cup walnut pieces
- ½ teaspoon kosher salt

FOR THE DRESSING:

- 3 tablespoons extra-virgin olive oil
- 1½ tablespoons champagne vinegar
- 1½ tablespoons Dijon mustard
- ¼ teaspoon kosher salt

FOR THE SALAD:

- 1 head red leaf lettuce, shredded into pieces
- 3 heads endive, ends trimmed and leaves separated
- 2 apples, cored and divided into thin wedges
- 1 (8-ounces) Camembert wheel, cut into thin wedges

Direction:

<u>To make the walnuts:</u>

1. Dissolve the butter in a skillet over medium-high heat. Stir in the sugar and cook until it dissolves. Add the walnuts and cook for about 5 minutes, stirring, until toasty. Season with salt and transfer to a plate to cool.

<u>To make the dressing:</u>

1. Whip the oil, vinegar, mustard, and salt in a large bowl until combined.

<u>To make the salad:</u>

1. Add the lettuce and endive to the bowl with the dressing and toss to coat. Transfer to a serving platter.
2. Decoratively arrange the apple and Camembert wedges over the lettuce and scatter the walnuts on top. Serve immediately.

3. Meal Prep Tip: Prepare the walnuts in advance — in fact, double the quantities and use them throughout the week to add a healthy crunch to salads, oats, or simply to enjoy as a snack.

Nutrition:

- **Calories:** 699;
- **Total fat:** 52 g;
- **Total carbs:** 44 g;
- **Cholesterol:** 60 mg;
- **Fiber:** 17 g;
- **Protein:** 23 g;
- **Sodium:** 1170 mg

16. <u>NORWEGIAN NIÇOISE SALAD: SMOKED SALMON, CUCUMBER, EGG, AND ASPARAGUS</u>

Easy/Gluten-free

Preparation Time: 20 minutes

Cooking Time: 5 minutes

Servings: 4

Ingredients:

FOR THE VINAIGRETTE:

- 3 tablespoons walnut oil
- 2 tablespoons champagne vinegar
- 1 tablespoon chopped fresh dill
- ½ teaspoon kosher salt

- ¼ teaspoon ground mustard
- Freshly ground black pepper

FOR THE SALAD:

- A handful of green beans, trimmed
- 1 (3- to 4-ounces) package spring greens
- 12 spears pickled asparagus
- 4 large soft-boiled eggs, halved
- 8 ounces smoked salmon, thinly sliced
- 1 cucumber, thinly sliced
- 1 lemon, quartered

Direction:

To make the dressing:

1. Mix vinegar, oil, dill, salt, ground mustard, and a few grinds of pepper in a small container until emulsified. Set aside.

To make the salad:

1. Start by blanching the green beans: Bring a pot of salted water to a boil. Drop in the beans. Cook or 1 to 2 minutes until they turn bright green, then immediately drain and rinse under cold water. Set aside.

2. Divide the spring greens among 4 plates. Toss each serving with dressing to taste. Arrange 3 asparagus spears, 1 egg, 2 ounces of salmon, one-fourth of the cucumber slices, and a lemon wedge on each plate. Serve immediately.

3. Meal Prep Tip: Prep each component in advance. Cook the eggs and blanch the beans a day in advance, make the dressing ahead of time, then simply dress and assemble the salads when it's time to serve.

Nutrition:

- **Calories:** 257;
- **Total fat:** 18 g;
- **Total carbs:** 6 g;
- **Cholesterol:** 199 mg;
- **Fiber:** 2 g;
- **Protein:** 19 g;
- **Sodium:** 603 mg

17. LOADED CAESAR SALAD WITH CRUNCHY CHICKPEAS

Easy/Gluten-free/Vegan

Preparation Time: 5 minutes

Cooking Time: 20 minutes

Servings: 6

Ingredient:

FOR THE CHICKPEAS:

- 2 (15-ounces) cans chickpeas, drained and rinsed
- 2 tablespoons extra-virgin olive oil
- 1 teaspoon kosher salt
- 1 teaspoon garlic powder
- 1 teaspoon onion powder
- 1 teaspoon dried oregano

FOR THE DRESSING:

- ½ cup of mayonnaise
- 2 tablespoons grated Parmesan cheese
- 2 tablespoons freshly squeezed lemon juice
- 1 clove garlic, peeled and smashed
- 1 teaspoon Dijon mustard
- ½ tablespoon Worcestershire sauce
- ½ tablespoon anchovy paste

FOR THE SALAD:

- 3 heads romaine lettuce, cut into bite-size pieces

Direction:

To make the chickpeas:

1. Preheat the oven to 450°F. Line a baking sheet with parchment paper.
2. Add the chickpeas, oil, salt, garlic powder, onion powder, and oregano in a small container. Scatter the coated chickpeas on the prepared baking sheet.
3. Roast for about 20 minutes, tossing occasionally until the chickpeas are golden and have a bit of crunch.

To make the dressing:

1. In a small bowl, whisk the mayonnaise, Parmesan, lemon juice, garlic, mustard, Worcestershire sauce, and anchovy paste until combined.

To make the salad:

1. Combine the lettuce and dressing in a large container. Toss to coat. Top with the roasted chickpeas and serve.
2. Cooking Tip: Don't wash out that bowl you used for the chickpeas — the remaining oil adds a great punch of flavor to blanched green beans or another simply cooked vegetable.

Nutrition:

- **Calories:** 367;
- **Total fat:** 22 g;
- **Total carbs:** 35 g;
- **Cholesterol:** 9 mg;
- **Protein:** 12 g;
- **Sodium:** 407mg

18. COLESLAW WORTH A SECOND HELPING

Easy/Gluten-free/Vegan

Preparation Time: 20 minutes

Cooking Time: 10 minutes

Servings: 6

Ingredients:

- 5 cups shredded cabbage
- 2 carrots, shredded
- ⅓ cup chopped fresh flat-leaf parsley
- ½ cup mayonnaise
- ½ cup sour cream
- 3 tablespoons apple cider vinegar
- 1 teaspoon kosher salt
- ½ teaspoon celery seed

Direction:

1. Add together the cabbage, carrots, and parsley in a large bowl.
2. Whisk together the mayonnaise, sour cream, vinegar, salt, and celery in a small bowl until smooth. Pour sauce over veggies and pour until covered. Transfer to a serving bowl and bake until ready to serve.

Nutrition:

- **Calories:** 192;
- **Total fat:** 18 g;
- **Total carbs:** 7 g;
- **Cholesterol:** 18 mg;
- **Protein:** 2 g;
- **Sodium:** 543 mg

19. ROMAINE LETTUCE AND RADICCHIOS MIX

Easy/Gluten-free/Vegan

Preparation time: 6 minutes

Cooking time: 0 minutes

Servings: 4

Ingredients:

- 2 tablespoons olive oil
- A pinch of salt and black pepper
- 2 spring onions, chopped
- 3 tablespoons Dijon mustard
- Juice of 1 lime
- ½ cup basil, chopped
- 4 cups romaine lettuce heads, chopped
- 3 radicchios, sliced

Directions:

In a salad bowl, blend the lettuce with the spring onions and the other ingredients, toss and serve.

Nutrition:

- **Calories:** 87,
- **Fats:** 2 g,
- **Fiber:** 1 g,
- **Carbs:** 1 g,
- **Protein:** 2 g

20. GREEK SALAD

Easy/Dairy-free/Vegan

Preparation Time: 15 Minutes

Cooking Time: 15 Minutes

Servings: 5

Ingredients:

FOR DRESSING:

- ½ teaspoon black pepper
- ¼ teaspoon salt
- ½ teaspoon oregano
- 1 tablespoon garlic powder
- 2 tablespoons Balsamic
- 1/3 cup olive oil

FOR SALAD:

- ½ cup sliced black olives
- ½ cup chopped parsley, fresh
- 1 small red onion, thin-sliced
- 1 cup cherry tomatoes, sliced
- 1 bell pepper, yellow, chunked
- 1 cucumber, peeled, quarter and slice
- 4 cups chopped romaine lettuce
- ½ teaspoon salt
- 2 tablespoons olive oil

Directions:

1. In a small container, join all of the ingredients for the dressing and let this set in the freezer while you make the salad.

2. To assemble the salad, mix together all the ingredients in a large-sized bowl and toss the veggies gently but thoroughly to mix.

3. Serve the salad with the dressing in amounts as desired

Nutrition:

- **Calories:** 234,
- **Fat:** 16.1 g,
- **Protein**: 5 g,

- **Carbs:** 48 g

21. ASPARAGUS AND SMOKED SALMON SALAD

Easy/Gluten-free/Vegan

Preparation time: 15 minutes

Cooking time: 10 minutes

Servings: 8

Ingredients:

- 1 lb. fresh asparagus, shaped and cut into 1-inch pieces
- 1/2 cup pecans, smashed into pieces
- 2 heads red leaf lettuce, washed and split
- 1/2 cup frozen green peas, thawed
- 1/4 lb. smoked salmon, cut into 1-inch chunks
- 1/4 cup olive oil
- 2 tablespoons. lemon juice
- 1 teaspoon Dijon mustard
- 1/2 teaspoon salt
- 1/4 teaspoon pepper

Directions:

1. Boil a pot of water. Stir in asparagus and cook for 5 minutes until tender. Let it drain; set aside.
2. In a skillet, cook the pecans over medium heat for 5 minutes, stirring constantly until lightly toasted.
3. Combine the asparagus, toasted pecans, salmon, peas, and red leaf lettuce and toss in a large bowl.
4. In another bowl, combine lemon juice, pepper, Dijon mustard, salt, and olive oil. You can coat the salad with the dressing or serve it on its side.

Nutrition:

- **Calories:** 159
- **Total Carbohydrate:** 7 g
- **Cholesterol:** 3 mg
- **Total Fat:** 12.9 g
- **Protein:** 6 g
- **Sodium:** 304 mg

22. SHRIMP COBB SALAD

Easy/Gluten-free/Vegan

Preparation time: 25 minutes

Cooking time: 10 minutes

Serving: 2

Ingredients:

- 4 slices center-cut bacon
- 1 lb. large shrimp, peeled and deveined
- 1/2 teaspoon ground paprika
- 1/4 teaspoon ground black pepper
- 1/4 teaspoon salt, divided
- 2 1/2 tablespoons. Fresh lemon juice
- 1 1/2 tablespoons. Extra-virgin olive oil
- 1/2 teaspoon whole-grain Dijon mustard
- 1 (10 oz.) package romaine lettuce hearts, chopped
- 2 cups cherry tomatoes, quartered
- 1 ripe avocado, cut into wedges
- 1 cup shredded carrots

Directions:

1. Cook the bacon for 4 minutes on each side in a large skillet over medium heat till crispy.
2. Take away from the skillet and place on paper towels; let cool for 5 minutes. Break the bacon into bits. Throw out most of the bacon fat, leaving behind only 1 tablespoon. in the skillet. Bring the skillet back to medium-high heat. Add black pepper and paprika to the shrimp for seasoning. Cook the shrimp around 2 minutes each side until it is opaque. Sprinkle with 1/8 teaspoon of salt for seasoning.
3. Combine the remaining 1/8 teaspoon of salt, mustard, olive oil, and lemon juice together in a small bowl. Stir in the romaine hearts.

4. On each serving plate, place on 1 and 1/2 cups of romaine lettuce. Add on top the same amounts of avocado, carrots, tomatoes, shrimp, and bacon.

Nutrition:

- **Calories: 528**
- **Total Carbohydrate:** 22.7 g
- **Cholesterol:** 365 mg
- **Total Fat:** 28.7 g
- **Protein:** 48.9 g
- **Sodium:** 1166 mg

23. TOAST WITH SMOKED SALMON, HERBED CREAM CHEESE, AND GREENS

Easy/Gluten-free/Vegan

Preparation time: 10 minutes

Cooking time: 5 minutes

Servings: 2

Ingredients:

FOR THE HERBED CREAM CHEESE:

- ¼ cup cream cheese, at room temperature
- 2 tablespoons chopped fresh flat-leaf parsley
- 2 tablespoons chopped fresh chives or sliced scallion
- ½ teaspoon garlic powder
- ¼ teaspoon kosher salt

FOR THE TOAST:

- 2 slices bread
- 4 ounces smoked salmon
- Small handful microgreens or sprouts
- 1 tablespoon capers, drained and rinsed
- ¼ small red onion, very thinly sliced

Directions:

To make the herbed cream cheese:

1. In a small container, put together the cream cheese, parsley, chives, garlic powder, and salt. Using a fork, mix until combined. Chill until ready to use.

To make the toast:

1. Toast the bread until golden. Spread the herbed cream cheese over each piece of toast, then top with the smoked salmon.
2. Garnish with the microgreens, capers, and red onion.

Nutrition:

- **Calories:** 194;
- **Total fat:** 8 g;
- **Cholesterol:** 26 mg;
- **Fiber:** 2 g;
- **Protein:** 12 g;
- **Sodium:** 227mg

24. <u>CRAB MELT WITH AVOCADO AND EGG</u>

Easy/Dairy-free/Vegan

Preparation time: 15 minutes

Cooking time: 15 minutes

Servings: 2

Ingredients:

- 2 English muffins, split
- 3 tablespoons butter, divided
- 2 tomatoes, cut into slices
- 1 (4-ounces) can lump crabmeat
- 6 ounces sliced or shredded cheddar cheese
- 4 large eggs
- Kosher salt
- 2 large avocados, halved, pitted, and cut into slices
- Microgreens, for garnish

Directions:

1. Preheat the broiler.
2. Toast the English muffin halves. Place the toasted halves, cut-side up, on a baking sheet.
3. Spread 1½ teaspoons of butter evenly over each half, allowing the butter to melt into the crevices. Top each with tomato slices, then divide the crab over each, and finish with the cheese.
4. Boil for about 4 minutes until the cheese melts.
5. Meanwhile, in a medium skillet over medium heat, melt the remaining 1 tablespoon of butter, swirling to coat the bottom of the skillet. Crack the eggs into the skillet, giving ample space for each. Sprinkle with

salt. Cook for about 3 minutes. Turn the eggs and cook the other side until the yolks are set to your liking. Place an egg on each English muffin half.

6. Top with avocado slices and microgreens.

Nutrition:

- **Calories:** 1221;
- **Total fat:** 84 g;
- **Cholesterol:** 94 mg;
- **Fiber:** 2 g;
- **Protein:** 12 g;
- **Sodium:** 888 mg

25. CRISPY POTATOES WITH SMOKED SALMON, KALE, AND HOLLANDAISE-STYLE SAUCE

Easy/Dairy-free/Vegan

Preparation time: 15 minutes

Cooking time: 15 minutes

Servings: 2

Ingredients:

- 2 tablespoons extra-virgin olive oil, plus additional for preparing the baking sheet
- ½ recipe roasted potatoes
- 8 ounces' mushrooms stemmed and sliced
- 1 garlic clove, minced
- 8 ounces' kale, thick stems removed, leaves cut into 2-inch pieces
- Kosher salt
- Freshly ground black pepper
- ½ recipe "Hollandaise-Style Sauce," at room temperature
- 8 ounces smoked salmon

Directions:

1. Preheat the oven to 400°F. Lightly coat a baking sheet with oil.
2. Place the roasted potatoes on the prepared baking sheet and heat until warm.
3. Heat the oil over medium heat until it shimmers. Add the mushrooms and sauté for about 4 minutes until softened. Add the garlic and cook for 30 seconds. Add the kale and sauté for about 5 minutes until wilted and soft. Season with salt and pepper.

4. In a large bowl, combine the warmed potatoes and the kale and mushroom mixture. Toss to combine. Divide between 2 plates and spoon the sauce on top.

5. Nestle the salmon next to the vegetables on each plate and serve.

Nutrition:

- **Calories:** 705;
- **Total fat:** 42g;
- **Cholesterol:** 47 mg;
- **Fiber:** 12 g;
- **Protein:** 15 g;
- **Sodium:** 427 mg

26. ROASTED VEGGIE BENEDICT WITH HOLLANDAISE-STYLE SAUCE AND ROASTED POTATOES

Medium/Gluten-free/Vegan

Preparation time: 30 minutes

Cooking time: 1 hour

Servings: 2

Ingredients:

FOR THE VEGETABLES AND EGGS:

- 4 tablespoons olive oil, divided, and more for preparing the baking sheets
- 1pound russet potatoes, with peels, cut into 1-inch pieces
- Kosher salt
- 1 (1-pound) eggplant cut into ¾-inch pieces
- 1 red bell pepper, cut into ¾-inch pieces
- 1 yellow onion, cut into ¾-inch wedges
- 4 garlic cloves, halved
- 1 tablespoon fresh rosemary leaves
- 4 large eggs

FOR THE HOLLANDAISE-STYLE SAUCE:

- 2 tablespoons butter
- 2 tablespoons all-purpose flour
- 1 cup milk
- 2 tablespoons freshly squeezed lemon juice
- 2 teaspoons Dijon mustard

- 1 teaspoon kosher salt
- ½ teaspoon soy sauce or tamari

FOR SERVING:

- 2 English muffins, split
- 2 tablespoons butter

Directions:

To make vegetables and eggs:

1. Preheat oven to 400 ° F. Gently coats 2 baking sheets with oil.
2. Place the potatoes in a large saucepan and add enough water to cover about 1 inch. Salt the water generously. Put the pot on top heat and bring to a boil. Adjust the heat, as needed, to maintain a simmer and cook for about 20 minutes until the potatoes are nearly fork-tender. Drain thoroughly in a colander.
3. While the potatoes boil, put the eggplant, bell pepper, onion, and garlic on one of the prepared baking sheets. Pour 2 tablespoons of oil over the vegetables. Sprinkle with the rosemary and 1 teaspoon of salt. Toss to coat.
4. Roast for 10 minutes. Turn the vegetables and roast for about 10 minutes more until the vegetables are soft and just starting to turn golden. Remove and keep warm.
5. Turn the drained potatoes out onto the second prepared baking sheet. Spill in the remaining 2 tablespoons of oil and salt. Get your coat.
6. Bake for about 25 minutes, turning each time, until golden brown and crisp.
7. Meanwhile, place a deep saucepan filled with about 3 inches of water over medium-high heat and simmer, adjusting the heat as needed. split the eggs into a small cup or plate and mix the eggs in the boiling water. Let them chase for a few minutes until the yolks start to come out. With a slotted spoon, gently scoop them up, set aside, and keep warm.

To make the hollandaise sauce:

1. Melt the butter over medium heat.
2. Add the flour and lightly beat until thickened.
3. Stirring constantly, gradually add the milk, allowing the stone to thicken before adding more milk. Put away from heat and mix in the lemon juice, mustard, salt, and soy sauce. Transfer to a serving bowl or refrigerate until ready to use.

To serve:

1. Toast the English muffin halves. Divide between 2 plates and spread each half with half of butter. Spoon the roasted vegetables over each and top with the poached eggs.
2. Finish with the sauce. Serve the potatoes on the side.

Nutrition:

- **Calories:** 1712;
- **Total fat:** 84 g;
- **Cholesterol:** 94 mg;
- **Fiber:** 2 g;
- **Protein:** 12 g;
- **Sodium:** 4887 mg

27. SEA BREEZE SALMON SALAD WITH MARGARITA DRESSING

Easy/Gluten-free/Vegan

Preparation time: 5 minutes

Cooking time: 15 minutes

Servings: 4

Ingredients:

- 1 pound fresh or frozen salmon fillets, cut into 4 pieces
- 5 tablespoons extra-virgin olive oil, divided
- 3 tablespoons freshly squeezed lime juice, divided
- 2 teaspoons Jamaican jerk seasoning
- 6 cups tightly packed mixed greens or spring mix lettuce
- 1 cup fresh strawberries, sliced
- 1 mango, diced
- 1 avocado, diced
- ¼ cup sliced or slivered almonds
- 1 tablespoon honey
- 1½ teaspoons ground cumin
- ⅛ teaspoon salt
- Fresh cilantro, for garnish

Directions:

1. Thaw the fish in cold water if using frozen, and preheat the oven to 400°F.
2. On the baking sheet, put the fillets and brush with 1 tablespoon of olive oil, then spray with 1 tablespoon of lime juice and sprinkle with the jerk seasoning. Broil the fish on the top rack for 12 to 14 minutes, or until it arrives at an internal temperature of 145°F, and the salmon flakes easily with a fork. Take away from the oven and allow to cool.

3. Meanwhile, in a large serving bowl, layer the salad greens followed by the strawberries, mango, avocado, and almonds. Toss gently to mix.

4. Beat together the remaining 4 tablespoons of olive oil, the remaining 2 tablespoons of lime juice, and the honey, cumin, and salt in a bowl.

5. To serve, arrange the salad mix on 4 plates. Top each salad with one salmon fillet, and gently flake apart. Add the dressing, and garnish with fresh cilantro, if desired.

Nutrition:

- **Calories:** 570;
- **Total fat:** 41 g;
- **Cholesterol:** 94 mg;
- **Fiber:** 2 g;
- **Protein:** 47 g;
- **Sodium:** 327 mg

28. CREAMY CRAWFISH BISQUE

Medium/Dairy-free/Vegan

Preparation time: 5 minutes

Cooking time: 35 minutes

Servings: 4

Ingredients:

- 2 tablespoons butter
- 1 yellow onion, diced
- ½ (6-ounces) can tomato paste, no salt added
- ½ teaspoon dried thyme
- 6 cups low-sodium vegetable or seafood stock
- 12 ounces' crawfish tail meat, divided
- 1 (14-ounces) block silken tofu, drained
- ½ cup 2% cottage cheese
- ¼ cup half-and-half
- 1 tablespoon freshly squeezed lemon juice
- Salt
- Freshly ground black pepper
- Scallions or fresh parsley, for garnish

Directions:

1. Over low heat in a large pot, dissolve the butter. Add the onion and cook for 5 minutes, or until the onions begin to soften.

2. Add the tomato paste and dried thyme, and stir to combine. Pour in the stock, scraping to deglaze the bottom of the pan. Bring to a simmer and add about half of the crawfish tails. Simmer for 15 to 20 minutes.

3. Add the silken tofu, and use an immersion blender to combine. If you don't have an immersion blender, carefully transfer to a blender and blend in batches with the lid let out to allow steam to escape.

4. Place the blended soup to the pan and cook for 5 minutes more. Stir in the cottage cheese, half-and-half, lemon juice, and the remaining crawfish tails. Cook it 5 minutes or more, till the crawfish tails curl and appear opaque, similar to cooked shrimp. Add salt and black pepper to taste. Ladle into four bowls, garnish with scallions or parsley, and serve.

Nutrition:

- **Calories:** 280;
- **Total fat:** 12 g;
- **Cholesterol:** 74 mg;
- **Fiber:** 2 g;
- **Protein:** 30 g;
- **Sodium:** 1080 mg

29. MASSAGED KALE SALAD WITH SESAME-LIME DRESSING

Easy/Gluten-Free/Vegan

Preparation time: 10 minutes

Cooking time: 8 minutes

Servings: 4

Ingredients:

- 6 cups fresh kale, tightly packed
- 1½ tablespoons sesame oil
- ¼ teaspoon coarse sea salt
- Juice of 1 lime
- 1 teaspoon honey
- 1½ cups shredded red cabbage
- 1 cup shelled edamame
- ½ cup slivered or sliced almonds

Directions:

1. Wash and dry the kale, stripping from stems if necessary. Chop or tear into bite-size pieces before measuring into a large mixing bowl.
2. Add the sesame oil and sea salt. Use clean, dry hands to massage the kale, working it between your fingers. Continue for 2 to 3 minutes, or until the kale is reduced to about half its original volume and becomes a deep green color.
3. In a small container, mix the lime juice and honey, and drizzle over the kale. Add the red cabbage, edamame, and almonds to the large mixing bowl, and toss to combine.

Nutrition:

- **Calories:** 250;
- **Total fat:** 17g;
- **Cholesterol:** 0 mg;
- **Protein:** 12 g;
- **Sodium:** 157 mg

30. SEAFOOD GUMBO-LAYA

Medium/Dairy-free/Vegan

Preparation time: 10 minutes

Cooking time: 30 minutes

Servings: 6

Ingredients:

- 2 tablespoons canola oil
- 3 celery stalks, diced
- 1 yellow onion, diced
- 1 green bell pepper, diced

- 3 garlic cloves, minced
- 2 bay leaves
- 1 teaspoon Creole seasoning
- ¼ teaspoon ground cayenne pepper
- ⅛ teaspoon freshly ground black pepper
- ½ (6-ounces) can tomato paste, no salt added
- 1 cup sliced frozen okra
- 1 (28-ounces) can crushed tomatoes
- 2 cups vegetable or seafood stock
- 1 pound peeled and deveined shrimp
- ½ pound bay scallops
- 6 cups cooked rice
- Fresh parsley, for garnish (optional)

Directions:

1. Over medium-high heat, heat the oil. Add the celery, onion, bell pepper, and garlic, and cook for 2 to 3 minutes, until it becomes fragrant, then add the bay leaves, Creole seasoning, cayenne pepper, and black pepper. Stir to combine, then add the tomato paste and cook for 2 to 3 minutes more.
2. Add the okra, tomatoes with their juices, and stock. Stir to combine and simmer, covered, stirring occasionally.
3. After 20 minutes, add the shrimp and scallops. Simmer for another 3 to 4 minutes, or until the seafood is fully cooked. The shrimp and scallops should be opaque.

Nutrition:

- **Calories:** 490;
- **Total fat:** 6 g;
- **Cholesterol:** 84 mg;
- **Fiber:** 2 g;
- **Protein:** 19 g;
- **Sodium:** 940 mg

31. CITRUS CAPRESE SALAD

Easy/Gluten-free/Vegan

Preparation time: 10 minutes

Cooking time: 8 minutes

Servings: 4

Ingredients:

- 2 cups fresh spinach, washed and dried
- 2 cups fresh arugula, washed and dried
- 1 red grapefruit
- 1 blood orange
- 1 Valencia or navel orange
- 8 ounces' fresh mozzarella
- ¼ cup fresh basil leaves washed and dried (optional)
- 4 tablespoons extra-virgin olive oil
- 2 tablespoons balsamic glaze
- Pinch salt
- Pinch freshly ground black pepper

Directions:

1. In a big salad bowl, arrange the spinach and arugula.
2. Using a chef's knife, slice the top and bottom from the grapefruit so it sits flat on a cutting board. Use the chef's knife to carefully slice away the peel and pith, leaving the flesh of the grapefruit intact. Turn the peeled grapefruit on its side and thinly slice. Add the grapefruit slices to the fresh greens.
3. Repeat with the blood orange and the Valencia orange, layering the slices randomly on the platter or in the bowl.
4. Slice the ball of mozzarella into similarly sized slices and layer among the citrus.
5. Chiffonade 8 to 10 large leaves of the basil and add to the salad.
6. Sprinkle with olive oil and balsamic glaze, and season with salt and pepper to taste. Serve immediately. If not serving right away, store prepped ingredients separately and do not dress the salad. Assemble upon serving to maintain freshness.

Nutrition:

- **Calories:** 270;
- **Total fat:** 16 g;
- **Cholesterol:** 3 5mg;
- **Fiber:** 2 g;
- **Protein:** 14 g;
- **Sodium:** 160 mg

32. SPRING GREENS PANZANELLA SALAD WITH SHRIMP

Medium/Gluten-free/Vegan

Preparation time: 5 minutes

Cooking time: 20 minutes

Servings: 4

Ingredients:

- ½ pound precooked frozen shrimp
- 3 slices day-old French or sourdough bread, cut into bite-size cubes
- 10 medium asparagus spears
- 6 cups loosely packed fresh spinach
- 4 Roma tomatoes, quartered or sliced
- ½ red onion, thinly sliced
- 4 tablespoons extra-virgin olive oil
- 2 tablespoons balsamic vinegar
- Pinch salt
- 1 avocado, diced
- About 5 large fresh basil leaves
- ½ cup shredded Parmesan cheese

Directions:

1. Thaw the shrimp by placing it in a large bowl of cold water. Preheat the oven to 300°F.
2. Line the bread on a baking sheet in a single layer, and toast until it becomes crunchy, 5 to 10 minutes total, flipping once during baking.
3. Meanwhile, on a second baking sheet, arrange the asparagus in a single layer. After removing the bread, raise the oven temperature to 375°F and roast the asparagus until it's a vibrant green color and is cooked through about 10 minutes.
4. In a salad bowl toss the spinach with the tomatoes, onion, olive oil, vinegar, and salt.
5. Add the avocado to the salad. Once the asparagus is roasted, cut into 1- to 2-inch pieces and add to the bowl. Mix to combine, then peel the shrimp and add to the salad. Top with the toasted bread. Toss one last time, then transfer to four bowls or plates.

Nutrition:

- **Calories:** 530;
- **Total fat:** 44 g;
- **Cholesterol:** 94 mg;
- **Protein:** 18 g;
- **Sodium:** 1080 mg

33. CRUNCHY CRUCIFEROUS CAESAR SALAD

Easy/Gluten-free/Vegan

Preparation time: 15 minutes

Cooking time: 5 minutes

Servings: 4

Ingredients:

- 1 bunch curly green kale
- 12 large Brussels sprouts
- 1 cup shredded red or green cabbage
- 1 tablespoon extra-virgin olive oil
- ¼ cup slivered almonds
- ⅔ cup shaved Parmesan cheese, divided
- 1 cup mayonnaise
- 2 tablespoons freshly squeezed lemon juice
- 2 garlic cloves, finely minced
- 1½ teaspoons anchovy paste
- 1½ teaspoons Dijon mustard
- 1 teaspoon Worcestershire sauce
- ⅛ teaspoon freshly ground black pepper

Directions:

1. Wash and dry the kale, Brussels sprouts, and cabbage. Strip the kale from the stems, and chop into bite-size pieces. Put the kale in a large mixing bowl, and sprinkle with the olive oil. Use clean, dry hands to massage the kale, working it between your fingers until it reduces in volume and becomes a deep, vibrant green, 2 to 3 minutes.

2. Trim the stems from the Brussels sprouts, and remove any damaged outer leaves. Halve each Brussels sprout and place flat-side down on a cutting board. Use a chef's knife to slice as thin as possible. Repeat with the remaining Brussels sprouts and add to the kale.

3. Add the cabbage, almonds, and ⅓ cup of Parmesan cheese to the mixing bowl, and toss to combine.

4. In a container, prepare the dressing by mixing the mayonnaise, lemon juice, garlic, anchovy paste, mustard, Worcestershire sauce, the remaining ⅓ cup of Parmesan cheese, and the black pepper together until well combined.

Nutrition:

- **Calories:** 440;

- **Total fat:** 32 g;
- **Cholesterol:** 35 mg;
- **Protein:** 14 g;
- **Sodium:** 427 mg

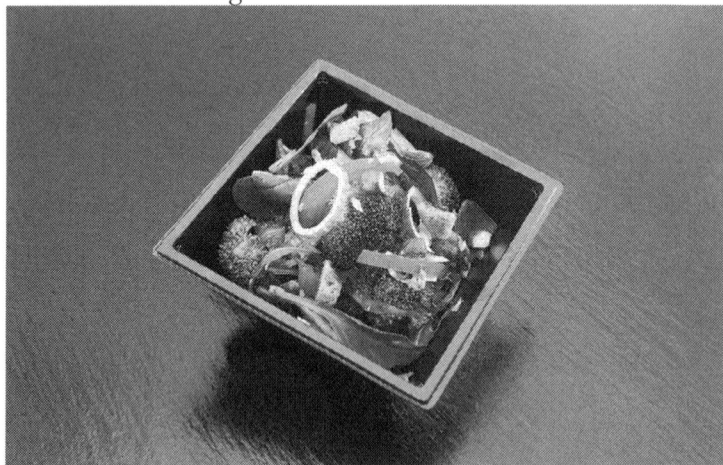

34. <u>GREEN BEAN NIÇOISE SALAD WITH TUNA</u>

Medium/Dairy-free/Vegan

Preparation time: 10 minutes

Cooking time: 30 minutes

Servings: 4

Ingredients:

- 8 ounces' small new potatoes
- 1-pound fresh green beans, trimmed
- 4 large eggs
- ¼ cup extra-virgin olive oil
- ½ red onion, finely chopped
- 1½ tablespoons freshly squeezed lemon juice
- 2 teaspoons Dijon mustard
- 1 teaspoon honey
- 1 tablespoon minced fresh dill, plus more for garnish
- Pinch salt
- Pinch freshly ground black pepper
- ¼ cup Kalamata or Niçoise olives pitted and halved
- 1 small bunch radishes, about 6 to 8 totals, trimmed and quartered

- 2 cans tuna packed in water, drained
- 2 tablespoons capers, drained (optional)

Directions:

1. Shred the potatoes and add them to a medium saucepan. Cover with water and bring to a boil. Cook the potatoes till they are soft when pierced with a fork, 12 to 15 minutes. Provide ice water in a big bowl and transfer the cooked potatoes to the ice bath. Let cool for 3 minutes, then remove and pat dry with a paper towel. Set aside.

2. Meanwhile, blanch the green beans by bringing a large saucepan of water to a boil. Add the green beans and cook 2 to 4 minutes, or until crisp-tender. Bring to the ice bath using tongs or a slotted spoon. Chill for 3 minutes, then remove and dry with a paper towel. Set aside.

3. Add the eggs to the same pot used for the green beans, and bring the water back to a boil. Boil the eggs for 8 to 10 minutes and then transfer them to the ice bath. Refresh with more ice if necessary. Let cool until cool, about 5 minutes. Peel the eggs and reserve.

4. In a bowl, prepare the dressing by mixing the olive oil, onion, lemon juice, mustard, honey, dill, salt, and pepper.

5. In a large bowl, toss the blanched green beans with about half of the dressing. Cut the frozen potatoes into large cubes and the eggs to the size you want. Arrange in a serving dish and then fill the potatoes, eggs, olives, radishes, and tuna.

Nutrition:

- **Calories:** 400;
- **Total fat:** 42 g;
- **Cholesterol:** 0 mg;
- **Fiber:** 2 g;
- **Protein:** 30 g;
- **Sodium:** 1677 mg

35. CREAMY CAULIFLOWER SOUP WITH SPICED CHICKPEAS

Easy/Gluten-free/Vegan

Preparation time: 10 minutes

Cooking time: 30 minutes

Servings: 4

Ingredients:

- Nonstick cooking spray (optional)
- 1 large head cauliflower

- 4 garlic cloves, minced
- 2 tablespoons extra-virgin olive oil, divided
- Pinch salt
- Pinch freshly ground black pepper
- 2 teaspoons ground cumin, divided
- 2 teaspoons red pepper flakes, divided, plus more for garnish
- 1 (14.5-ounces) can chickpeas, drained and rinsed
- ½ yellow onion, diced
- 3 cups low-sodium vegetable stock
- 1 (14-ounces) block silken tofu, drained
- ½ cup half-and-half
- Fresh thyme, for garnish (optional)

Directions:

1. Preheat the oven to 400°F. String a baking sheet with baking paper or spray with nonstick cooking spray.
2. Toss the cauliflower with the garlic, 1 tablespoon of olive oil, the salt, and black pepper, and 1 teaspoon of cumin and red pepper flakes. Arrange on the baking sheet in a single layer and bake on the upper or middle rack for 30 minutes, turning once, if you want, even for browning.
3. Line a second baking sheet with parchment or spray with nonstick cooking spray. Pat the drained chickpeas dry, then add the remaining tablespoon of olive oil and the remaining teaspoon of cumin and crushed red pepper. Organize in a single layer. Add to the oven on the bottom baking rack and bake for 20 minutes, or until crisp and baked on the outside.
4. Meanwhile, add the onion to a large saucepan. Add the stock, and cook over low heat.
5. When the cauliflower and chickpeas are cooked, remove them from the oven. Set aside the chickpeas along with a small roasted cauliflower broth for garnish. Add the remaining cauliflower and silken tofu to the boiling broth. Reduce heat and stir to combine.
6. Using a blender, blend until thick and creamy, about 2 minutes. Add half and half and mix again until smooth. If you don't have an immersion blender, transfer it to a blender and mix carefully in batches with the vented lid to release steam.
7. Serve the soup in four bowls with a quarter of the crispy chickpeas and reserved cauliflower florets in each, along with fresh thyme and additional red pepper flakes, if desired.

Nutrition:

- **Calories:** 320;
- **Total fat:** 22 g;
- **Cholesterol:** 94 mg;

- **Fiber:** 2 g;
- **Protein:** 15 g;
- **Sodium:** 327 mg

36. SMOKED OYSTER & CLAM CHOWDER

Medium/Gluten-free/Vegan

Preparation time: 10 minutes

Cooking time: 30 minutes

Servings: 4

Ingredients:

- 1 tablespoon canola oil
- 1 sweet or yellow onion, diced
- 3 celery stalks, cut into ¼-inch slices
- 2 or 3 rosemary sprigs
- 2 bay leaves
- 1 cup dry white wine
- 4 cups of seafood stock
- 3 large white potatoes, diced (peel if desired)
- 2 (6-ounces) cans clams
- 1 (3-ounces) can smoked oysters
- 1 cup frozen or canned sweet corn kernels
- 8 ounces half-and-half
- Salt
- Freshly ground black pepper
- Fresh rosemary, for garnish (optional)

Directions:

1. Over medium heat, heat a large pot. Add the oil. Once the skillet is shiny, add the onion, celery, rosemary, and bay leaves. Sauté 5 to 8 minutes or until onion is translucent. Add the white wine and stir, scraping to peel the bottom of the pan. Cook for another 3 minutes.
2. Add the seafood broth and potatoes. Boil, then reduce the heat and poach for 15 minutes or until the potatoes are soft. Meanwhile, we drain and chop the mussels and oysters.
3. After 10 minutes, carefully pour half of the soup, including the liquid, into a blender. Vent the lid to allow steam to escape and mix until smooth. Place the puree back in the pot or Dutch oven and stir to thicken.

4. Add the clams, oysters, corn, and half-and-half. Simmer for 8 minutes more. Add salt and pepper, and serve with fresh rosemary, if desired.

Nutrition:

- **Calories:** 490;
- **Total fat:** 14 g;
- **Cholesterol:** 34 mg;
- **Fiber:** 2 g;
- **Protein:** 21 g;
- **Sodium:** 157 mg

37. <u>FISHERMAN'S STEW IN THE SLOW COOKER</u>

Medium/Dairy-free/Vegan

Preparation time: 10 minutes

Cooking time: 4 to 6 hours

Servings: 4

Ingredients:

- 1 (28-ounces) can diced tomatoes
- 1 (6-ounces) can tomato paste, with no salt
- 4 cups of seafood stock
- 3 garlic cloves, minced
- ½ pound new potatoes, scrubbed
- 1 sweet or yellow onion, diced
- 1 large celery stalk, cut
- 1 teaspoon dried thyme

- 1 teaspoon dried oregano
- 1 teaspoon dried basil
- 2 bay leaves
- 1 pound mixed frozen seafood (shrimp, scallops, mussels, crab, lobster)
- 1 bunch scallions, thinly sliced, for garnish
- 4 slices toasted French or sourdough bread

Directions:

1. In the slow cooker, combine the tomatoes and their juices, tomato paste, seafood stock, garlic, potatoes, onion, celery, thyme, oregano, basil, and bay leaves. Gently stir until the tomato paste is incorporated into the mixture. Cook on high for 3 hours or on low for 4 to 5 hours, or until the potatoes are tender.
2. Meanwhile, thaw the seafood in a cold-water bath, and rinse under cold running water. Open the cooker and add the seafood. Cook for 30 to 60 minutes longer, or until the seafood is fully cooked.
3. Remove the bay leaves, ladle into four bowls, and garnish with the scallions.

Nutrition:

- **Calories:** 420;
- **Total fat:** 3 g;
- **Cholesterol:** 84 mg;
- **Fiber:** 2 g;
- **Protein:** 28 g;
- **Sodium:** 197 mg

38. VEGETARIAN CHILI WITH BUTTERNUT SQUASH

Medium/Dairy-free/Vegan

Preparation time: 10 minutes

Cooking time: 5 hours

Servings: 4

Ingredients:

- 1 red onion, diced
- 1 green bell pepper, diced
- 1 red bell pepper, diced
- 2½ cups peeled and cubed butternut squash
- 1 (28-ounces) can crushed tomatoes
- 3 garlic cloves, minced
- 1 tablespoon chili powder

- ½ tablespoon ground cumin
- ½ teaspoon ground cayenne pepper
- ½ teaspoon ground cinnamon
- ¼ teaspoon salt
- 1 (15.5-ounces) can black beans, drained and rinsed
- 1 (15.5-ounces) can kidney beans, drained and rinsed
- 2 cups of water
- 1 cup uncooked quinoa
- Sour cream, for garnish (optional)

Directions:

1. In the slow cooker, combine the onion, green and red bell peppers, squash, tomatoes with their juices, garlic, chili powder, cumin, cayenne pepper, cinnamon, salt, black and kidney beans, water, and quinoa, then stir gently to combine. Cook on high for 4 to 5 hours or low for 6 to 7 hours.
2. Turn the slow cooker to warm until ready to serve. Top each bowl with sour cream, if desired.

Nutrition:

- **Calories:** 470;
- **Total fat:** 11 g;
- **Cholesterol:** 94 mg;
- **Fiber:** 2 g;
- **Protein:** 17 g;
- **Sodium:** 227 mg

Chapter 6. VEGETARIAN MAINS- PLANT-BASED

39. FARRO BOWL WITH MUSHROOMS, BLUEBERRIES, GOAT CHEESE, AND WALNUTS

Easy/Gluten-free/Vegan

Preparation time: 20 minutes

Cooking time: 30 minutes

Servings: 4

Ingredients:

- 1 cup uncooked pearled farro
- 2 cups of water
- 2 tablespoons sherry vinegar
- 1 teaspoon kosher salt
- 3 tablespoons walnut oil (look for roasted walnut oil for extra flavor)
- 2 tablespoons extra-virgin olive oil
- 8 ounces cremini mushrooms, sliced
- 2 garlic cloves, crushed
- 1 cup walnut halves and pieces, roughly chopped
- 1 cup fresh blueberries
- 4 ounces' fresh goat cheese (chèvre), crumbled
- 1 tablespoon chopped fresh dill

Directions:

1. Rinse the farro, then place it in a medium saucepan with the water. Bring to a boil over high heat. Lower the heat, cover the pan, and simmer for about 20 minutes until tender. Drain any excess water.
2. Meanwhile, in a small bowl, make the dressing by combining the vinegar and salt. Gradually whisk in the walnut oil to emulsify. Pour this over the farro and stir to combine. Set aside.
3. In a large skillet over medium-high heat, warm the olive oil until it shimmers. Add the mushrooms and sauté for about 4 minutes. Add the garlic and cook for 1 minute more until the mushrooms are cooked. Transfer the mixture to a plate and set aside.
4. Using the same skillet over medium heat, toast the walnuts until fragrant, then transfer to a small bowl.
5. To assemble, divide the dressed farro among 4 bowls. Arrange the sautéed mushrooms, toasted walnuts, blueberries, goat cheese, and dill over each.

Nutrition:

- **Calories:** 639;
- **Total fat:** 43 g;
- **Cholesterol:** 94 mg;
- **Fiber:** 2 g;
- **Protein:** 17 g;
- **Sodium:** 327 mg

40. QUINOA BOWLS WITH CURRIED CAULIFLOWER AND SPINACH

Easy/Gluten-free/Vegan

Preparation time: 20 minutes

Cooking time: 30 minutes

Servings: 4

Ingredients:

- 1¾ cups water
- 1 cup quinoa
- 1 large head cauliflower, cut into florets
- 2 tablespoons olive oil
- 1 tablespoon curry powder
- ¼ teaspoon kosher salt
- Juice of 1 lemon
- Grated zest of 1 lemon
- 4 cups fresh baby spinach leaves
- ¼ cup chopped fresh cilantro
- ½ cup sliced or slivered almonds

Directions: Preheat the oven to 400°F.

1. In a medium pot over high heat, bring the water to a boil. Rinse the quinoa to remove the saponin coating, which can taste bitter, then add the quinoa to the boiling water. Reduce the heat to maintain a simmer, cover the pot, and cook for about 20 minutes until the water is absorbed and the quinoa is fluffy. Remove from the heat and set aside.

2. Meanwhile, on a baking sheet, toss together the cauliflower, oil, curry powder, and salt.

3. Roast for about 20 minutes, turning once or twice until the cauliflower is tender and starting to turn golden.

4. Transfer the cooked quinoa to a large bowl. Add the lemon juice and lemon zest, stirring thoroughly to combine. Once the quinoa is mostly room temperature, add the spinach leaves and cilantro and stir again.

5. Divide the quinoa between 4 bowls. Top with the cauliflower and almonds.

Nutrition:

- **Calories:** 361;
- **Total fat:** 16 g;
- **Cholesterol:** 0 mg;
- **Fiber:** 2 g;
- **Protein:** 14 g;
- **Sodium:** 327 mg

41. <u>ROASTED VEGGIE–LOADED QUINOA BOWL</u>

Easy/Gluten-free/Vegan

Preparation time: 25 minutes

Cooking time: 30 minutes

Servings: 4

Ingredients:

FOR THE ROASTED VEGETABLES:

- 3 tablespoons olive oil, plus more for preparing the baking sheet
- 1 eggplant, cut into 1½-inch pieces
- 1 zucchini, cut into 1-inch pieces
- 1 red bell pepper, cut into 1-inch pieces
- 1 yellow onion, cut into 1-inch wedges

- 4 garlic cloves, halved
- 1 tablespoon fresh rosemary leaves, plus sprigs for garnish
- 1 teaspoon kosher salt

FOR THE QUINOA:

- 1¾ cups water
- 1 cup quinoa
- 1 tablespoon olive oil
- ½ teaspoon kosher salt

Directions:

To make the roasted vegetables:

1. Preheat the oven to 400°F. Lightly coat a baking sheet with oil.

2. Place the eggplant, zucchini, red bell pepper, onion, and garlic on the prepared baking sheet. Pour the oil over, sprinkle with the rosemary and salt, and toss to coat.

3. Roast for about 20 minutes, turning once or twice until the vegetables are soft and just starting to turn golden.

To make the quinoa:

1. Meanwhile, in a medium pot over high heat, bring the water to a boil. Rinse the quinoa to remove the saponin coating, which can taste bitter, then add the quinoa to the boiling water. Reduce the heat to maintain a simmer, cover the pot, and cook for about 20 minutes until the water is absorbed and the quinoa is fluffy. Remove from the heat, and stir in the oil and salt.

2. To assemble, spoon the quinoa into 4 bowls and top with the vegetables. Garnish with rosemary sprigs.

Nutrition:

- **Calories:** 341;
- **Total fat:** 16 g;
- **Cholesterol:** 0 mg;
- **Fiber:** 2 g;
- **Protein**: 9 g;
- **Sodium:** 884 mg

42. CAPONATA WITH EGGPLANT, ZUCCHINI, TOMATOES, AND ROASTED PEPPER

Easy/Gluten-free/Vegan

Preparation time: 15 minutes

Cooking time: 30 minutes

Servings: 6 *(double)*

Ingredients:

- ¼ cup olive oil
- 2 onions, cut into slices
- 1 (1-pound) eggplant, cut into 1-inch pieces
- 1 pound zucchini, cut into 1-inch pieces
- 2 red bell peppers, cut into 1-inch pieces
- 1 (32-ounces) can diced tomatoes
- 2 garlic cloves, thinly sliced
- 2 tablespoons capers, drained and rinsed
- 2 teaspoons kosher salt
- 1 to 2 tablespoons red wine vinegar
- 1 teaspoon sugar

Directions:

1. In a large pot over medium to medium-high heat, heat the oil until it shimmers. Add the onions and sauté for about 5 minutes until translucent.
2. Add the eggplant, zucchini, and red bell peppers. Cook, stirring frequently, for about 20 minutes until tender.
3. Pour in the tomatoes. Add the garlic and capers and bring to a simmer. Taste and add salt, as needed, along with the vinegar and sugar.

Nutrition:

- **Calories:** 186;
- **Total fat:** 10 g;
- **Cholesterol:** 0 mg;
- **Fiber:** 2 g;
- **Protein:** 5 g;

- **Sodium:** 1080 mg

43. <u>THAI-INSPIRED GREEN CURRY WITH LOADS OF VEGETABLES</u>

Easy/Gluten-free/Vegan

Preparation time: 20 minutes

Cooking time: 25 minutes

Servings: 4

Ingredients:

FOR THE CURRY PASTE:

- 1 (4-inches) piece lemongrass, tough outer layer removed and discarded, inner part roughly chopped
- 1 jalapeño pepper, seeded
- 1 small shallot, roughly chopped
- 4 garlic cloves, peeled
- ½ cup packed fresh cilantro, roughly chopped
- 3 tablespoons freshly squeezed lime juice

FOR THE CURRY:

- 2 tablespoons canola oil, plus more as needed
- 1 (12-ounces) package tofu, cut into 1-inch cubes
- 2 cups low-sodium vegetable broth
- 1 cup trimmed green beans
- 1 red bell pepper, cut into slices
- ½ large eggplant, cut into 1½-inch pieces
- 1 zucchini, cut into 1-inch pieces

- 1 (14-ounces) can unsweetened coconut milk
- Cooked brown rice, for serving
- Fresh basil leaves, for garnish

Directions:

To make the curry paste:

In a food processor, combine the lemongrass, jalapeño, shallot, garlic, cilantro, and lime juice. Blitz until all the ingredients are chopped and combined. Set aside.

To make the curry:

1. Preheat the oven to 200°F.
2. In a large pan over medium-high heat, heat the oil until it shimmers. Add the tofu and fry until golden and crisp. Carefully transfer the tofu to a heatproof plate and place it in the oven to keep warm.
3. Return the pan to medium-high heat and add a little more oil, if needed. Add the curry paste and cook for about 1 minute, stirring until the spices and ingredients are fragrant.
4. Add the vegetable broth, green beans, red bell pepper, eggplant, and zucchini. Bring it to a simmer. Cook for about 10 minutes until the vegetables are tender. Stir in the coconut milk and the fried tofu.
5. Serve over brown rice and garnish with fresh basil leaves.

Nutrition:

- **Calories:** 551;
- **Total fat:** 38 g;
- **Cholesterol:** 94 mg;
- **Fiber:** 2 g;
- **Protein:** 23 g;
- **Sodium:** 167 mg

44. VEGETABLE GARDEN LASAGNA

Easy/Gluten-free/Vegan

Preparation time: 45 minutes

Cooking time: 1 hour

Servings: 8

Ingredients:

- 2 tablespoons olive oil, plus more for preparing the baking dish
- 14 lasagna noodles
- 1 onion, chopped
- 5 garlic cloves, crushed

- 2 heads broccoli, cut into ½-inch pieces
- 2 zucchinis, halved lengthwise, then crosswise into ¼-inch slices
- 2 carrots, diced
- 1 red bell pepper, diced
- 1 (24-ounces) jar seasoned pasta sauce, divided
- ½ teaspoon red pepper flakes
- 1 (15-ounces) container ricotta
- 1 cup grated Parmesan cheese
- 2 large eggs
- Kosher salt, to taste
- 12 ounces fresh baby spinach, finely chopped
- 8 ounces shredded mozzarella cheese, divided

Directions:

1. Preheat the oven to 375°F. Lightly coat a 9-by-13-inch baking dish with oil.

2. Cook the noodles according to the package directions. Drain.

3. Meanwhile, in a large skillet over medium-high heat, heat the oil. Add the onion and sauté for about 5 minutes until translucent. Add the garlic and give it another 30 seconds. Add the broccoli, zucchini, carrots, and red bell pepper. Sauté for about 10 minutes until the vegetables are tender. Reserve ½ cup of pasta sauce and pour the remaining into the skillet. Add the red pepper flakes and remove from the heat.

4. In a medium bowl, stir together the ricotta, Parmesan, eggs, salt, and spinach.

5. Cover the bottom of the pan with a thin layer of the reserved pasta sauce. Place half the noodles side by side to cover the bottom. Spread half the ricotta mixture over the noodles, then half the vegetables, and about two-thirds of the mozzarella. Repeat: sauce, noodles, ricotta, and vegetables, finishing with the remaining mozzarella cheese. Cover the dish with aluminum foil.

6. Bake for 30 minutes. Remove the foil and bake for about 10 minutes more until the cheese on top is golden and bubbly.

Nutrition:

- **Calories:** 570;
- **Total fat:** 24 g;
- **Cholesterol:** 0 mg;
- **Fiber:** 2 g;
- **Protein:** 32 g;

- **Sodium:** 327 mg

45. CREAMY RICE WITH PORTABELLA MUSHROOMS

Easy/Gluten-free/Vegan

Preparation time: 20 minutes

Cooking time: 1 hour

Servings: 4

Ingredients:

- 1¾ cups water
- 1 cup uncooked rice, rinsed
- 3 tablespoons olive oil, plus more for preparing the baking sheet
- 2 portabella mushrooms, cut into ½-inch slices
- 1 pound cremini mushrooms or button mushrooms, sliced
- 3 garlic cloves, crushed
- 2 teaspoons fresh thyme leaves, plus sprigs for garnish
- 3 tablespoons plant-based butter alternative
- 3 tablespoons all-purpose flour
- 2 cups low-sodium vegetable broth
- 1 teaspoon kosher salt

Directions:

1. In a pot over high heat, combine the water and the rice. Salt the water and bring to a boil. Reduce the heat to simmer, cover the pot, and cook for 45 minutes. Remove from the heat, fluff with a fork, cover the pot, and let steam for 10 minutes more.

2. Meanwhile, preheat the oven to 400°F. Lightly coat a baking sheet with oil.

3. Put the portabella mushrooms on the prepared baking sheet.

4. Bake for 10 minutes. Flip the mushrooms and bake for about 20 minutes more until tender. Set aside and cover with aluminum foil to keep warm.

5. In a large skillet over medium-high heat, heat the oil. Add the cremini mushrooms and sauté for 5 to 7 minutes until golden brown. Add the garlic and thyme leaves and remove the skillet from the heat.

6. In a pot over medium heat, melt the butter alternative. Add the flour and whisk until it absorbs the butter, then, a little at a time, add the vegetable broth, whisking constantly, waiting for the mixture to seize up before each addition. Add the salt, then pour this into the skillet with the cremini mushrooms.

7. Add the rice to the skillet and stir to combine. Transfer to a serving platter and top with the roasted portabella slices. Garnish with thyme sprigs.

Nutrition:

- **Calories:** 421;
- **Total fat:** 20 g;
- **Cholesterol:** 14 mg;
- **Fiber:** 2 g;
- **Protein:** 10 g;
- **Sodium:** 841 mg

46. SMASHED POTATOES WITH CHICKPEAS AND ROMESCO SAUCE

Easy/Gluten-free/Vegan

Preparation time: 30 minutes

Cooking time: 45 minutes

Servings: 4 to 6

Ingredients:

- 2 pounds' baby potatoes, scrubbed
- ½ cup olive oil, divided
- Kosher salt
- 2 red bell peppers, stemmed, seeded, and halved lengthwise
- 2 (15-ounces) cans chickpeas, drained and rinsed
- ½ cup sliced almonds
- 1 garlic clove, peeled
- 2 tablespoons tomato paste
- 1 tablespoon freshly squeezed lemon juice

- 1 teaspoon fresh rosemary leaves
- ¼ teaspoon smoked paprika
- Chopped fresh herbs, for garnish

Directions:

1. Bring a large pot of generously salted water to a boil over high heat. Add the potatoes and cook for about 20 minutes, or until tender. Drain.
2. Meanwhile, preheat the oven to 425°F. Line a baking sheet with parchment paper.
3. Put the boiled potatoes on the prepared baking sheet. Using the bottom of a glass, smash each potato, then drizzle with ¼ cup of oil and season with salt.
4. Roast on the middle rack for about 20 minutes until golden and crispy.
5. While the potatoes bake, place the red bell pepper halves, skin-side up, on the top oven rack. Roast for 10 minutes until they begin to char. Remove them from the oven and place them in a clean paper bag or cover with aluminum foil and let cool for about 10 minutes until they can be safely handled. Peel off and discard the skins.
6. Arrange the mashed potatoes on a serving platter and scatter the chickpeas over top.
7. Place the peeled peppers in a food processor and add the almonds, remaining ¼ cup of oil, garlic, tomato paste, lemon juice, 1 teaspoon of salt, the rosemary, and paprika. Whirl until smooth. Taste and add more salt, if needed. Spoon the romesco sauce over the potatoes and chickpeas and garnish with fresh herbs.

Nutrition:

- **Calories:** 351;
- **Total fat:** 34 g;
- **Cholesterol:** 0 mg;
- **Fiber:** 2 g;
- **Protein:** 1 6g;
- **Sodium**: 845 mg

47. <u>EASY VEGETABLE STIR-FRY</u>

Easy/Gluten-free/Vegan

Preparation time: 20 minutes

Cooking time: 10 minutes

Servings: 4

Ingredients:

FOR THE STIR-FRY SAUCE:

- ½ cup soy sauce or tamari

- ¼ cup low-sodium vegetable broth
- ¼ cup sesame oil
- 1 tablespoon cornstarch
- 1 tablespoon light brown sugar

FOR THE STIR-FRY:

1. 2 tablespoons vegetable oil
2. 1 red bell pepper, cut into ½-inch slices
3. 8 ounces cremini mushrooms, sliced
4. 1 onion, chopped
5. 1 cup snap peas, trimmed
6. ½ cup shelled edamame
7. 1 (8-ounces) can water chestnuts, drained
8. 2 garlic cloves, minced
9. 1 (1-inch) piece fresh ginger, peeled and minced
10. 1 cup cherry tomatoes, halved
11. Cooked rice, for serving
12. Sesame seeds, for serving
13. Small handful fresh basil leaves, torn into pieces

Directions:

To make the stir-fry sauce:

1. In a small bowl, whisk the soy sauce, vegetable broth, sesame oil, cornstarch, and brown sugar until smooth. Set aside.

To make the stir-fry:

1. In a large wok or skillet over medium-high heat, heat the vegetable oil. Add the red bell pepper, mushrooms, and onion. Cook, stirring, for 1 to 2 minutes.
2. Add the snap peas, edamame, and water chestnuts. Cook for 1 minute more. Toss in the garlic, ginger, and cherry tomatoes. Cook, stirring, for about 30 seconds.
3. Pour in the stir-fry sauce and cook for about 3 minutes until thickened. Serve with rice and garnish with sesame seeds and fresh basil.

Nutrition:

- **Calories:** 473;
- **Total fat:** 22 g;
- **Cholesterol:** 94 mg;

- **Fiber:** 2 g;
- **Protein:** 12 g;
- **Sodium:** 1127 mg

48. <u>BOOSTED VEGETABLE FRIED RICE</u>

Easy/Gluten-free/Vegan

Preparation time: 15 minutes

Cooking time: 15 minutes

Servings: 4 to 6

Ingredients:

- 4 large eggs
- 1 tablespoon water
- ⅛ teaspoon kosher salt
- 2 tablespoons vegetable oil
- 1 tablespoon sesame oil
- 1 cup frozen peas, thawed
- 1 bunch scallions (about 6), thinly sliced, white and light-green parts separated from the green tops
- 2 garlic cloves, minced
- 1 (1-inch) piece fresh ginger, peeled and minced
- 4 cups cooked brown rice, cold
- 1 (14-ounces) can chickpeas, drained and rinsed
- 3 to 4 tablespoons soy sauce or tamari
- 1 cup shredded red cabbage
- ½ cup shredded carrot
- ¼ cup fresh cilantro leaves

Directions:

1. In a small bowl, whisk the eggs, water, and the salt like you are making scrambled eggs.
2. In a large skillet over medium heat, heat the vegetable oil, swirling it to coat the bottom and sides of the skillet. Pour in the eggs and cook until set. Transfer to a cutting board and cut into ¼-inch pieces.
3. Return the skillet to the heat and add the sesame oil. Add the peas, the white and light-green scallion parts, garlic, and ginger. Cook for about 2 minutes.
4. Stir in the rice, chickpeas, soy sauce, red cabbage, carrot, dark-green scallion parts, and the cooked egg. Cook, stirring for 3 to 4 minutes, or until the rice is heated and the ingredients combined. Garnish with cilantro.

egg + peas at the end

81

Nutrition:

- **Calories:** 551;
- **Total fat:** 19 g;
- **Cholesterol:** 0 mg;
- **Fiber:** 2 g;
- **Protein:** 20 g;
- **Sodium:** 1106 mg

49. SIMPLIFIED PAD THAI

Easy/Gluten-free/Vegan

Preparation time: 10 minutes

Cooking time: 15 minutes

Servings: 4

Ingredients:

- 8 ounces wide rice noodles
- 1 tablespoon canola oil
- 1 tablespoon peanut oil
- 1 (12-ounces) package tofu, cut into 1-inch cubes
- 2 garlic cloves, crushed
- 2 tablespoons freshly squeezed lime juice
- 1 tablespoon tamari
- 1 tablespoon Thai fish sauce (nam pla)
- 1 tablespoon light brown sugar

- ½ cup shredded carrot
- ½ cup bean sprouts
- ¼ cup chopped roasted unsalted peanuts
- 3 scallions, thinly sliced

Directions:

1. Cook the rice noodles according to the package directions.
2. In a large skillet over medium heat, heat the canola oil and peanut oil. Add the tofu and garlic and fry for 3 to 4 minutes per side until the tofu is golden and crisp.
3. In a small bowl, whisk the lime juice, tamari, fish sauce, and brown sugar to blend. Pour this sauce into the skillet and add the drained pasta and carrot. Stir to combine. Transfer to a serving dish and top with the bean sprouts, peanuts, and scallions.

Nutrition:

- **Calories:** 351;
- **Total fat:** 18 g;
- **Cholesterol:** 0 mg;
- **Fiber:** 2 g;
- **Protein:** 17 g;
- **Sodium:** 327mg

50. WHOLE-WHEAT PASTA WITH SAUTÉED GREENS

Easy/Gluten-free/Vegan

Preparation time: 10 minutes

Cooking time: 25 minutes

Servings: 4

Ingredients:

- 1-pound whole-wheat pasta
- ½ cup extra-virgin olive oil, divided
- 4 garlic cloves, minced
- 2 large bunches broccolini
- ½ teaspoon kosher salt
- ½ teaspoon red pepper flakes
- 1 cup hazelnuts, chopped
- 2 tablespoons dry white wine
- ½ cup chopped fresh flat-leaf parsley

- Lemon wedges, for serving

Directions:

1. Cook the pasta according to the package instructions. Reserve ½ cup of the cooking water and drain. Set aside.

2. In a large skillet over medium heat, heat ¼ cup of oil. Add the garlic and let it bathe for about 30 seconds until fragrant. Add the broccolini. Cover the skillet and let the broccolini cook for about 4 minutes to get slightly tender. Remove the lid, increase the heat, and add the salt and red pepper flakes. Sauté until the broccolini has crisped a bit. Transfer the broccolini to a bowl.

3. Return the skillet to the heat and add the remaining ¼ cup of oil to heat. Add the hazelnuts and the white wine. Cook for 1 minute or so until the hazelnuts just start to turn golden, then add the pasta and parsley and stir to coat.

4. To serve, mound a serving of pasta on each plate and arrange some of the broccolini on top. Serve with lemon wedges for squeezing.

Nutrition:

- **Calories:** 427;
- **Total fat:** 47 g;
- **Cholesterol:** 0 mg;
- **Fiber:** 2 g;
- **Protein:** 30 g;
- **Sodium:** 327 mg

51. PENNE ALL' ARRABBIATA

Easy/Gluten-free/Vegan

Preparation time: 10 minutes

Cooking time: 30 minutes

Servings: 4

Ingredients:

- 1 pound penne pasta
- 2 tablespoons olive oil
- 4 garlic cloves, crushed
- 2 tablespoons dry white wine
- 1 (14-ounces) can crushed tomatoes
- ½ teaspoon red pepper flakes, plus more for serving
- 1 (4-ounces) can sliced black olives

- Kosher salt
- Fresh basil leaves, cut into chiffonade
- Freshly grated Parmesan cheese or Pecorino Romano cheese, for serving

Directions:

1. Cook the pasta according to the package directions.
2. Meanwhile, in a large pot over medium heat, heat the oil. Add the garlic and let it sizzle for about 30 seconds until richly fragrant. Add the white wine and let the alcohol evaporate for 1 to 2 minutes, then pour in the tomatoes and add the red pepper flakes. Bring the sauce to a simmer and cook for about 20 minutes until the flavors are deeply melded and the sauce has thickened slightly. Stir in the olives and season with salt.
3. Add the pasta to the sauce and stir to coat. Serve with basil leaves, cheese, and additional red pepper flakes in case anyone wants a little extra heat.

Nutrition:

- **Calories:** 551;
- **Total fat:** 13 g;
- **Cholesterol:** 0 mg;
- **Fiber: 2 g;**
- **Protein:** 18 g;
- **Sodium:** 527 mg

52. SWEET POTATOES WITH LOADED VEGETABLE TOPPINGS

Easy/Gluten-free/Vegan

Preparation time: 15 minutes

Cooking time: 45 minutes

Servings: 2

Ingredients:

- 1 large sweet potato
- 1 (14-ounces) can chickpeas, drained and rinsed
- ¼ cup chopped fresh cilantro
- ¼ cup extra-virgin olive oil
- 1 teaspoon ground cumin
- ½ teaspoon kosher salt
- ½ cup pico de gallo or chunky salsa, for serving
- Queso fresco, for serving

Directions:

1. Preheat the oven to 450°F.
2. Prick the sweet potato all over with a fork, then place it directly on the oven rack. Roast for about 45 minutes, turning a time or two, as needed, or until tender throughout when pierced with a fork or knife.
3. Carefully transfer the sweet potato to a cutting board. Using a sharp knife, halve the sweet potato lengthwise. Score the flesh several times and mash it a bit with a fork, creating lots of places for the flavorful toppings to seep into. Place one half, skin-side down, on each of 2 plates.
4. In a medium bowl, stir together the chickpeas, cilantro, oil, cumin, and salt. Spoon the mixture over the sweet potatoes, letting the topping spill onto the plate. Top with pico de gallo and crumbled queso fresco.

Nutrition:

- **Calories:** 541;
- **Total fat:** 31 g;
- **Cholesterol:** 0 mg;
- **Fiber:** 2 g;
- **Protein:** 14 g;
- **Sodium:** 827 mg

53. GREENS AND MUSHROOMS OVER BEANS

Easy/Gluten-free/Vegan

Preparation time: 10 minutes

Cooking time: 10 minutes

Servings: 2

Ingredients:

- 1 tablespoon olive oil

- 1 onion, sliced
- 8 ounces' mushrooms, sliced
- Kosher salt
- 1 (14-ounces) can cannellini beans, drained and rinsed
- 1 bunch collard greens or Swiss chard, roughly chopped
- Nutritional yeast, for serving (optional)

Directions:

1. In a medium pan over medium-high heat, heat the olive oil. Add the onion and sauté for 3 to 4 minutes until translucent. Transfer the onion to a plate.

2. Return the pan to the heat. Add the mushrooms with a bit of salt and cook or 5 to 7 minutes until they're golden brown and tender.

3. Add the cannellini beans and the greens to the pan with a splash of water. Cover the pan, allowing the greens to wilt as they steam for a minute or two. Stir in the onion. Season to taste with salt. Serve, sprinkled with nutritional yeast (if using).

Nutrition:

- **Calories:** 321;
- **Total fat:** 9 g;
- **Cholesterol:** 0 mg;
- **Fiber:** 2 g;
- **Protein:** 19 g;
- **Sodium:** 527mg

Chapter 7. SEAFOOD MAINS

54. GARLIC AND HERB SPAGHETTI WITH CRAB

Easy/Dairy-free/Vegan

Preparation time: 15 minutes

Cooking time: 15 minutes

Servings: 4

Ingredients:

- ½ cup white wine
- 2 (1½-pounds) whole cooked Dungeness crabs, rinsed
- 1 (12-ounces) package dried spaghetti
- ½ cup olive oil
- 8 garlic cloves, thinly sliced
- 1 cup hazelnuts, finely chopped
- 1 teaspoon red pepper flakes
- 1 bunch finely chopped fresh parsley
- 1 (7-ounces) wedge Parmesan cheese, grated or finely shredded
- 1 teaspoon kosher salt
- 1 lemon, cut into wedges, for serving

Directions:

1. Place a metal steamer basket into a large pot big enough to hold the crabs. Pour in water until it reaches the bottom of the basket. Bring to a boil over high heat, then reduce the heat to maintain a simmer and pour in the wine.

2. Nestle the crabs in the basket and cover with a lid. Steam for 3 to 5 minutes until heated through. Carefully remove the crabs with tongs and transfer to a plate, tented with aluminum foil until the pasta is done.

3. While the crab steams, cook the pasta according to the package instructions. Reserve ½ cup of the cooking water, then drain.

4. While the pasta cooks, pour the oil into a large pan over medium heat and let it warm. Add the garlic and let it bathe in the warm oil for 3 to 4 minutes until richly fragrant but not yet turning brown. Add the hazelnuts and red pepper flakes and remove from the heat.

5. Transfer the pasta to the pot and give it a quick stir to coat with the oil, then add the parsley, Parmesan, and salt. Stir, adding the reserved cooking water a little at a time, using just enough to help melt the

cheese and create a sauce that coats the pasta. Transfer to plates or a serving platter and top with the crab. Serve with lemon wedges.

Nutrition:

- **Calories:** 551;
- **Total fat:** 51g;
- **Cholesterol:** 105 mg;
- **Fiber:** 2 g;
- **Protein:** 23 g;
- **Sodium:** 1127 mg

55. <u>BUTTERY SHRIMP SCAMPI PASTA WITH GARLICKY TOMATOES AND HERBS</u>

Easy/Gluten-free/Vegan

Preparation time: 15 minutes

Cooking time: 15 minutes

Servings: 4

Ingredients:

- 1 (12-ounces) package dried spaghetti
- 6 tablespoons (¾ stick) salted butter
- 2 tablespoons olive oil
- 6 garlic cloves, minced
- 2 pounds large uncooked shrimp, peeled and deveined

- ¼ cup dry white wine, such as Pinot Gris
- 2 tomatoes, cut into ½-inch pieces
- ½ cup chopped fresh parsley
- ¼ cup freshly squeezed lemon juice
- Lemon wedges, for serving
- Red pepper flakes, for serving

Directions:

1. Cook the spaghetti according to the package instructions. Drain.
2. While the pasta cooks, in a large skillet over medium-high heat, melt the butter, then pour in the oil. Add the garlic and cook for about 30 seconds until fragrant.
3. Add the shrimp and cook for about 3 minutes until pink and firm. Using a slotted spoon, remove the shrimp and place them on a plate, tenting with aluminum foil to keep warm.
4. Pour the wine into the skillet and increase the heat to high, letting the alcohol evaporate for 1 to 2 minutes. Add the tomatoes, parsley, and lemon juice, then tip the shrimp and their juices back in. Add the pasta and stir everything to coat. Serve with lemon wedges and a bowl of red pepper flakes on the side.

Nutrition:

- **Calories:** 451;
- **Total fat:** 28 g;
- **Cholesterol:** 332 mg;
- **Fiber:** 2 g;
- **Protein:** 44 g;
- **Sodium:** 1106 mg

56. SIMPLY POACHED PRAWNS WITH HERB SAUCE

Easy/Gluten-free/Vegan

Preparation time: 10 minutes

Cooking time: 8 minutes

Servings: 4

Ingredients:

- 2 pounds unpeeled prawns
- ½ cup extra-virgin olive oil
- ½ teaspoon kosher salt
- ½ cup fresh flat-leaf parsley, chopped
- ¼ cup almonds

- 3 tablespoons chopped fresh mint
- 1 tablespoon chopped fresh chives

Directions:

1. Bring a large pot of generously salted water to a boil over high heat. Add the prawns. Adjust the heat to maintain a simmer and cook for about 3 minutes depending on their size, until the shrimp turn opaque and pink.
2. Meanwhile, in a food processor, combine the oil, salt, parsley, almonds, mint, and chives. Whirl until the nuts are pulverized and the ingredients have combined into a thick green sauce. Transfer to a small bowl.
3. To serve, mound the prawns on a platter alongside the bowl of sauce.

Nutrition:

- **Calories:** 451;
- **Total fat:** 32 g;
- **Cholesterol:** 286 mg;
- **Fiber:** 2 g;
- **Protein:** 32 g;
- **Sodium:** 1127 mg

57. <u>SIMPLY BROILED HALIBUT WITH A FRESH CILANTRO-CORN SALAD</u>

Easy/Dairy-free/Vegan

Preparation time: 15 minutes

Cooking time: 15 minutes

Servings: 4

Ingredients:

- 1pound halibut fillets rinsed and patted dry
- ¼ cup olive oil, plus more for brushing the fish
- Kosher salt
- 4 ears fresh corn, kernels cut from the cob
- 1pint cherry tomatoes halved crosswise
- ½ shallot, minced
- ¼ cup chopped fresh cilantro leaves, plus a few leaves for garnish
- ¼ cup freshly squeezed lime juice
- 1 teaspoon ground cumin
- ½ teaspoon ground coriander
- 2 avocados, peeled, halved, pitted, and cut into slices

Directions:

1. Preheat the broiler.

2. Place the halibut on a broiler pan, skin-side down, and brush the top with oil. Sprinkle salt evenly over the top.

3. Roast for about 7 minutes, or until the fish reaches 145°F, depending on the thickness of the fish. When done, it should flake easily with a fork and be opaque inside.

4. While the fish cooks, in a large bowl, stir together the corn, tomatoes, shallot, cilantro, oil, lime juice, cumin, and coriander to combine. Season with salt. Distribute the salad among 4 plates and arrange the avocado slices attractively over each salad.

5. Divide the halibut into 4 portions and nestle them against the salad.

Nutrition:

- **Calories:** 451;
- **Total fat:** 31 g;
- **Cholesterol:** 94 mg;
- **Fiber:** 2 g;
- **Protein:** 29 g;
- **Sodium:** 129 mg

58. WHITE WINE–POACHED COD WITH CREAMY DILL SAUCE

Easy/Dairy-free/Vegan

Preparation time: 10 minutes

Cooking time: 15 minutes

Servings: 4

Ingredients:

FOR THE SAUCE:

- ¼ cup Crème Fraîche
- ¼ cup chopped fresh dill
- ½ teaspoon freshly squeezed lemon juice, plus more for seasoning
- ⅛ teaspoon kosher salt, plus more for seasoning

FOR THE FISH:

- 3 cups of water
- 1 cup dry white wine
- 2 tablespoons fresh rosemary leaves

- 1 bay leaf
- 1 teaspoon kosher salt
- 1½ pounds cod fillets, rinsed, cut to fit in a large skillet

Directions:

To make the sauce

In a small bowl, stir together the Crème Fraîche, dill, lemon juice, and salt. Taste and adjust seasonings, as needed. Set aside.

To make the fish

1. In a large skillet over medium-high heat, combine the water, rosemary, bay leaf, and salt. Bring to a low boil.
2. Add the cod and adjust the heat to maintain a simmer. Cook for about 7 minutes, depending on thickness until the cod is cooked through and begins to flake. Carefully transfer the fish to a platter. Serve the fish with the sauce drizzled over top or in a ramekin on the side.

Nutrition:

- **Calories:** 317;
- **Total fat:** 4 g;
- **Cholesterol:** 24 mg;
- **Fiber:** 2 g;
- **Protein:** 31 g;
- **Sodium:** 227 mg

59. SCANDI-STYLE FISH CAKES WITH RÉMOULADE

Easy/Gluten-free/Vegan

Preparation time: 20 minutes

Cooking time: 20 minutes

Servings: 4

Ingredients:

FOR THE RÉMOULADE:

- 1 cup mayonnaise
- ½ cup minced dill pickles or cornichons
- ¼ cup lightly packed chopped fresh herbs (e.g., parsley and dill)
- 2 tablespoons capers, drained and rinsed
- 1 teaspoon Dijon mustard
- 1 tablespoon freshly squeezed lemon juice

- ¼ teaspoon kosher salt

FOR THE FISH CAKES:

- 1½ pounds cod fillets, cut into small pieces
- 1 teaspoon kosher salt
- 1 small onion, roughly chopped
- 3 tablespoons melted butter plus 2 tablespoons at room temperature
- 2 large eggs
- 2 scallions, white and light-green parts only, chopped
- ¼ cup finely chopped fresh parsley
- ¼ cup finely chopped fresh dill
- 2 tablespoons freshly squeezed lemon juice
- 2 tablespoons all-purpose flour
- 2 tablespoons vegetable oil

Directions:

To make the rémoulade:

1. In a medium bowl, stir together the mayonnaise, pickles, herbs, capers, mustard, lemon juice, and salt. Cover and refrigerate until ready to serve.

To make the fish cakes:

1. Put the cod on a paper-towel-lined plate and lightly sprinkle with salt. Let sit for 10 minutes. Using a paper towel, wipe away the moisture and any excess salt. You're drawing out the moisture here rather than seasoning the fish.
2. In a food processor, finely chop the onion. Add the cod and pulse to break down the fish a bit. Add 3 tablespoons of melted butter, the eggs, scallions, parsley, dill, and lemon juice. Process until almost smooth. Add the flour and process until smooth and combined. (You can make the fish cakes up to this point, 1 to 2 hours in advance, just keep the mixture refrigerated.)
3. Wet your hands and form the fish mixture into 12 balls. Slightly flatten each and place the cakes on a paper-towel-lined plate while you work so they continue to release excess moisture.
4. In a large skillet over medium heat, heat the oil and the remaining 2 tablespoons of butter. Carefully place the patties into the pan, working in batches if needed. Cook for about 5 minutes per side until golden outside and cooked through. Serve with the rémoulade.

Nutrition:

- **Calories:** 485;
- **Total fat:** 34 g;

- **Cholesterol:** 34 mg;
- **Fiber:** 2 g;
- **Protein:** 32 g;
- **Sodium:** 427mg

60. ROCKFISH WITH SWEET-AND-SOUR TOMATO AND BELL PEPPER SAUCE AND PASTA

Medium/Dairy-free/Vegan

Preparation time: 10 minutes

Cooking time: 25 minutes

Servings: 4

Ingredients:

- ½ cup olive oil plus 1 tablespoon, plus more for preparing the pan and fish
- 2 pounds' rockfish fillets rinsed and patted dry
- Kosher salt
- 6 garlic cloves, thinly sliced
- 6 baby bell peppers, any color, thinly sliced
- 3 tablespoons fresh rosemary leaves
- 1 cup cherry tomatoes, halved lengthwise
- 1 pound dried capellini pasta

Directions:

1. Preheat the broiler. Lightly coat a broiler pan with oil.

2. Place the fish on the prepared broiler pan. Brush it with oil and scatter salt on top.

3. Boil for about 5 minutes until opaque and cooked through. When done, the fish should flake easily with a fork.

4. While the fish cooks, in a large skillet over medium heat, heat ½ cup of oil. Add the garlic, letting it bathe in the oil for about 1 minute until deeply fragrant but barely taking on any color.

5. Tip in the bell peppers and rosemary. Cook, stirring occasionally, for 2 to 3 minutes.

6. Add the tomatoes. Cook for 1 minute. Using the back of a wooden spoon, lightly smash the tomatoes. Season with salt to taste. Remove from the heat and keep warm.

7. Cook the pasta according to the package directions. Drain and toss with the remaining 1 tablespoon of oil.

8. Distribute the pasta among 4 plates and top with the fish. Spoon the pepper-and-tomato sauce over each and serve.

Nutrition:

- **Calories:** 916;
- **Total fat:** 32 g;
- **Cholesterol:** 64 mg;
- **Fiber:** 2 g;
- **Protein:** 58 g;
- **Sodium:** 227mg

61. OVEN-BAKED FISH AND CHIPS

Medium/Dairy-free/Vegan

Preparation time: 1 hour

Cooking time: 40 minutes

Servings: 4

Ingredients:

- 2 pounds' russet potatoes cut lengthwise into ½-inch wedges
- ¼ cup olive oil
- 2 tablespoons kosher salt, plus more for seasoning
- 1 cup all-purpose flour
- 2 large egg whites, lightly beaten
- 1½ cups panko bread crumbs
- 2 pounds' cod fillets or other whitefish
- 1 recipe Coleslaw Worth a Second Helping

- Tartar sauce or Rémoulade, for serving
- Malt vinegar, for serving
- Lemon wedges, for serving
- Ketchup, for serving

Directions:

1. Put the potato wedges in a large bowl and cover with water. Let them soak for about 30 minutes, then drain and pat dry with a paper towel.
2. While the potatoes soak, preheat the oven to 400°F. Line a large baking sheet with parchment paper.
3. Put the potatoes on the prepared baking sheet and toss them with the oil and salt. Arrange the potatoes in a single layer.
4. Roast for 10 minutes. Flip the potatoes and roast for 10 minutes more until golden and crisp.
5. While the potatoes roast put the flour in one shallow bowl. In a second shallow bowl, whisk the egg whites and put the panko in a third bowl.
6. Pat the fish dry and season with salt. Dredge the fish in the flour, the egg whites, and the panko.
7. Remove the baking sheet from the oven. Using a heatproof spatula, scoot the potatoes off to the side and make room for the fish. Arrange the fish next to the potatoes in a single layer. Roast for about 18 minutes, depending on the thickness of the fish, flipping the fish once until golden and crispy and the internal temperature reaches 145°F.
8. Serve with the coleslaw, tartar sauce, vinegar, lemon wedges, and ketchup.

Nutrition:

- **Calories:** 603;
- **Total fat:** 14 g;
- **Cholesterol:** 94 mg;
- **Fiber:** 2 g;
- **Protein:** 50 g;
- **Sodium:** 2007mg

62. PAN-SEARED BLACK COD WITH FENNEL-BLACKBERRY SALAD, HERBED CUCUMBER PUREE, AND HOMEMADE MAYONNAISE

Medium/Gluten-free/Vegan

Preparation time: 45 minutes

Cooking time: 10 to 15 minutes

Servings: 4

Ingredients:

FOR THE FISH:

- 1½ pounds black cod, skin on, halved as needed to fit in the pan
- Kosher salt
- 1 to 2 tablespoons olive oil

FOR THE SALAD:

- 1 fennel bulb with greens
- 2 tablespoons best-quality extra-virgin olive oil
- 2 tablespoons freshly squeezed lemon juice
- ¼ teaspoon kosher salt
- 4 radishes, cut into eighths
- 6 ounces' fresh blackberries

FOR THE CUCUMBER PUREE:

- 1 cucumber, peeled and halved lengthwise
- 6 tablespoons extra-virgin olive oil
- ¼ cup fresh parsley
- 2 tablespoons freshly squeezed lemon juice
- 1 tablespoon garlic oil
- ½ teaspoon kosher salt, plus more for seasoning

FOR THE MAYONNAISE:

- 3 large egg yolks
- 1 teaspoon ground mustard (I use Coleman's)
- 1 cup extra-virgin olive oil
- 2 tablespoons freshly squeezed lemon juice
- 1 teaspoon kosher salt, plus more for seasoning
- Dash freshly ground black pepper, plus more for seasoning

Directions:

To start the fish:

1. Rinse the black cod and pat it dry. Season with salt and let sit while you prepare the salad and sauces.

To make the salad:

1. Cut the stalks from the fennel bulb and remove the wispy fronds, roughly chopping them and setting them aside. Cut the bulb as thinly as possible, ideally using a mandoline.
2. In a medium bowl, whisk the oil, lemon juice, and salt to combine.
3. Add the sliced fennel and the chopped fronds, and toss to coat.

4. Add the radishes and blackberries. Set aside.

To make the cucumber puree:

1. Using the tip of a spoon, scrape the seeds from the cucumber and cut the flesh into 1-inch pieces. Transfer to a high-powered blender and add the oil, parsley, lemon juice, garlic oil, and salt. Blend until smooth. Taste and adjust the seasoning, as needed.

To make the mayonnaise:

1. In a food processor, whirl together the egg yolks and ground mustard.

2. With the machine running, add the oil, a little at a time, letting the oil slowly drip into the egg yolks to emulsify (if your food processor has a pusher with a small hole in the bottom, use this to help moderate the speed, but still take care not to add too much oil at once).

3. Once the oil is incorporated and emulsified, add the lemon juice, salt, and pepper and give it another quick whirl. Taste and adjust the seasonings, as needed. Refrigerate while you prepare the fish.

To finish the fish:

1. In a large skillet over medium-high heat, heat the oil. Add the cod, flesh-side down, and cook for about 5 minutes until golden brown. Gently flip the fish — it will be very delicate at this point — and cook on the skin side for about 5 minutes more until the fish is opaque and cooked through.

2. Arrange the fennel salad on each of 4 plates. Arrange the cod in the middle. Spoon a dollop of mayonnaise on top and drizzle the cucumber sauce around.

Nutrition:

- **Calories:** 251;
- **Total fat:** 44 g;
- **Cholesterol:** 84 mg;
- **Fiber:** 2 g;
- **Protein:** 28 g;
- **Sodium:** 1127 mg

63. PAN-FRIED TROUT WITH BUTTER BEANS AND ROSEMARY BROTH

Easy/Gluten-free/Vegan

Preparation time: 25 minutes

Cooking time: 10 minutes

Servings: 2

Ingredients:

- 1 whole trout, cleaned
- Kosher salt

- 2 tablespoons olive oil
- 1 cup dry white wine
- Juice of ½ large lemon
- 4 thin lemon slices
- 3 garlic cloves, crushed
- 3 rosemary sprigs
- 1 (14-ounces) can butter beans, drained and rinsed
- 3 tablespoons butter

Directions:
1. Rinse the trout and pat it dry. Halve it lengthwise and sprinkle salt over the flesh of each portion.
2. In a large pan over medium heat, heat the oil. Add the trout, flesh-side down. Cook for about 4 minutes until the flesh is turning golden. Carefully flip the fish skin-side down.
3. Pour in the white wine and lemon juice and nestle the lemon slices, garlic cloves, and rosemary sprigs in with the fish. Cook for 3 minutes, or until the fish is cooked through. Using a slotted spoon, gently remove the trout and set aside.
4. Add the beans and butter to the pan and bring to a simmer. Cook for about 2 minutes until the beans are heated through and the butter is melted.
5. Spoon the beans into 2 large bowls and pour the cooking liquid over. Top with the trout and garnish with the rosemary sprigs and lemon slices from the pan.

Nutrition:
- **Calories:** 621;
- **Total fat:** 35 g;
- **Cholesterol:** 94 mg;
- **Fiber:** 2 g;
- **Protein:** 25 g;
- **Sodium:** 527 mg

64. A SEATTLE GRILLED SALMON DINNER

Easy/Gluten-free/Vegan

Preparation time: 10 minutes

Cooking time: 10 minutes

Servings: 4

Ingredients:

FOR THE SAUCE:

- 3 tablespoons sour cream
- 1 tablespoon mayonnaise
- 1 teaspoon freshly squeezed lemon juice
- ¼ teaspoon kosher salt
- 2 tablespoons chopped fresh dill

FOR THE SALMON:

- 1 (2-pound) skin-on salmon fillet
- Extra-virgin olive oil
- Kosher salt
- Lemon wedges, for serving

Directions:

To make the sauce:

1. In a small bowl, whisk the sour cream, mayonnaise, lemon juice, and salt until smooth. Stir in the dill. Refrigerate until needed.

To make the salmon:

1. Preheat a grill to high.
2. Rinse the salmon and pat it dry, then brush it with oil and sprinkle with salt. Place the salmon on the grill, flesh-side down, and sear for 4 minutes. Reduce the heat a bit and flip the salmon, continuing to grill for about 4 minutes more, or until the fish is cooked to 145°F. (The exact cooking time will vary, depending on the thickness of the fish.) Alternatively, you can bake or broil the salmon.
3. Serve the fish on a platter with the sauce and lemon wedges alongside it.

Nutrition:

- **Calories:** 471;
- **Total fat:** 30 g;
- **Cholesterol:** 120 mg;
- **Fiber:** 2g;
- **Protein:** 43 g;
- **Sodium:** 327 mg

65. BAKED SALMON WITH FRENCH-STYLE LENTIL AND SPINACH SALAD

Medium/Gluten-free/Vegan

Preparation time: 20 minutes

Cooking time: 45 minutes

Servings: 4

Ingredients:

- ½ cup extra-virgin olive oil, divided, plus more for preparing the baking dish
- 1 cup dried French green lentils, rinsed and picked over for debris
- 4 cups of water
- 2 bay leaves
- 3 tablespoons sherry wine vinegar
- 2 teaspoons Dijon mustard
- 1 teaspoon kosher salt plus ¼ teaspoon
- 3 tablespoons minced shallot
- ½ cup chopped fresh Italian parsley
- 4 cups fresh baby spinach
- 4 (6-ounces) wild Alaskan salmon fillets
- Pinch freshly ground black pepper
- ¼ teaspoon ground fennel seed (or fennel pollen)
- 12 cornichons

Directions:

1. Preheat the oven to 400°F. Brush an ovenproof baking dish large enough to hold the salmon with oil.
2. In a medium saucepan over high heat, combine the lentils, water, and bay leaves. Bring the water to a boil. Lower the heat to maintain a simmer, cover the pan, and simmer for about 20 minutes until the lentils are tender. Drain any excess water, remove and discard the bay leaves, and transfer the lentils to a large bowl.
3. While the lentils cook, in a small bowl, whisk the vinegar, mustard, and 1 teaspoon of salt. While whisking constantly, gradually pour in about 7 tablespoons of oil, whisking to emulsify.
4. Add the shallot, parsley, and three-quarters of the dressing to the lentils and stir until the lentils are coated with the dressing. Add the spinach, working in batches, stirring until it wilts. Keep warm until ready to serve.
5. Wipe the salmon dry with a paper towel. Set the salmon in the prepared baking dish, skin-side down. Brush with the remaining 1 tablespoon of oil, then sprinkle with the remaining ¼ teaspoon of salt, the pepper, and fennel seed.
6. Bake for about 20 minutes until just cooked through.
7. Divide the salmon among 4 plates. Spoon mounds of lentil salad alongside. Offer the remaining dressing and the cornichons on the side for serving.

Nutrition:

- **Calories:** 680;
- **Total fat:** 39 g;
- **Cholesterol:** 94 mg;
- **Fiber:** 2 g;
- **Protein:** 49 g;
- **Sodium:** 1217 mg

66. WEEKNIGHT SALMON WITH CHARD, MUSHROOMS, AND BEANS

Easy/Dairy-free/Vegan

Preparation time: 15 minutes

Cooking time: 20 minutes

Servings: 4

Ingredients:

- Olive oil
- 4 (6-ounces) wild Alaskan salmon fillets
- 2 garlic cloves, crushed
- 8 ounces' mushrooms, sliced
- 1 bunch chard, cut into 1-inch lengths
- Red pepper flakes, for seasoning
- 1 (14-ounces) can cannellini beans, drained and rinsed
- Kosher salt
- Freshly ground black pepper

Directions:

1. Preheat the oven to 400°F. Brush a baking sheet with oil.
2. Place the salmon on the prepared baking sheet and brush with oil.
3. Bake for about 20 minutes until cooked through.
4. Meanwhile, in a large pan over medium-high heat, heat a tablespoon of oil. Add the garlic and sauté for about 30 seconds until fragrant. Add the mushrooms and sauté for about 5 to 7 minutes more until softened.
5. Stir in the chard and red pepper flakes, stirring to coat. Cover the pan and steam the chard for 2 to 3 minutes, stirring occasionally while you check on its progress until wilted.
6. Stir in the cannellini beans and season with salt and pepper.
7. Divide the beans and greens among 4 plates and top with the salmon fillets.

Nutrition:

- **Calories:** 351;
- **Total fat:** 13 g;
- **Cholesterol:** 94 mg;
- **Fiber:** 2 g;
- **Protein:** 40 g;
- **Sodium:** 327 mg

67. STEAMED MUSSELS WITH LEMONGRASS BROTH AND COCONUT MILK

Medium/Dairy-free/Vegan

Preparation time: 20 minutes

Cooking time: 40 minutes

Servings: 4

Ingredients:

- 1 lemongrass stalk, tough outer part removed
- 2 cups low-sodium vegetable broth
- 1 (1½-inch) piece galangal, thinly sliced
- Grated zest of 1 lime
- 3 tablespoons olive oil
- 1 leek, rinsed well, thinly sliced (about 1 cup)
- 3 garlic cloves, thinly sliced
- 12 ounces mixed mushrooms (such as cremini and shiitake), sliced
- Kosher salt
- 1 (14-ounces) can coconut milk
- 1 cup dry white wine
- 4 pounds' mussels, scrubbed and debearded
- 2 to 3 tablespoons fish sauce, plus more for seasoning
- Juice of 1 lime, plus more for seasoning
- 1 cup chopped fresh cilantro leaves

Directions:

1. Halve the lemongrass lengthwise, bash it with a rolling pin or meat mallet a few times, then cut it into 1-inch lengths.

2. In a medium pot over medium-high heat, combine the vegetable broth, lemongrass, galangal, and lime zest. Bring to a simmer and cook for about 15 minutes, then strain and discard the solids. Set the broth aside.

3. In a large pot over medium heat, heat the oil until it shimmers. Add the leek and cook, stirring, for about 3 minutes until softened. Add the garlic and cook, stirring, for 1 minute more. Add the mushrooms, season with a little salt, and cook, stirring regularly, for about 7 minutes until the mushrooms are soft.

4. Pour in the lemongrass broth, coconut milk, and white wine. Bring the liquid to a simmer.

5. Add the mussels and cover the pot, letting them steam for a few minutes until they open. Discard any mussels that do not open.

6. Add the fish sauce and lime juice and give the broth a taste, adding a little more of these if needed. Garnish with cilantro.

Nutrition:

- **Calories:** 451;
- **Total fat:** 36 g;
- **Cholesterol:** 46 mg;
- **Fiber:** 2 g;
- **Protein:** 41g;
- **Sodium:** 1267 mg

68. SHEET PAN SALMON WITH POTATOES AND ASPARAGUS

Easy/Dairy-free/Vegan

Preparation time: 15 minutes

Cooking time: 25 minutes

Servings: 4

Ingredients:

- 2 tablespoons olive oil, plus more for preparing the pan and fish
- 4 (6-ounces) wild Alaskan salmon fillets
- Kosher salt
- 1-pound red potatoes, cut into 1-inch pieces
- 1 bunch asparagus, bottom ends trimmed
- 1 teaspoon herbs de Provence
- 1 cup cherry tomatoes or grape tomatoes, halved crosswise

Directions:

1. Preheat the oven to 400°F. Brush a large sheet pan with oil.

2. Place the salmon on one side of the prepared pan and brush it with oil.

3. Place the potatoes and the asparagus on the other side of the pan, tossing with the oil and herbs de Provence, and sprinkling with salt.

4. Bake for about 20 minutes, turning the vegetables every once in a while, until the salmon is cooked throughout (145°F) and the potatoes and asparagus are tender and golden. Remove any elements early, if needed, to avoid overcooking; the potatoes, for example, may take longer than the other items.

5. Transfer the potatoes and asparagus to a platter and scatter the tomatoes over this. Top with the salmon and serve.

Nutrition:

- **Calories:** 351;
- **Total fat:** 17 g;
- **Cholesterol:** 94 mg;
- **Fiber:** 2 g;
- **Protein:** 37 g;
- **Sodium:** 137 mg

Chapter 8. GLUTEN-FREE

69. CREAMY PEACH ICE POPS

Easy/Gluten-free

Preparation time: 10 minutes plus 5 hours to freeze

Cooking time: 5 minutes

Servings: 8

Ingredients:

- 1 (14-ounces) can light coconut milk
- 2 peaches, peeled, pitted, and roughly chopped
- ¼ cup honey
- Pinch cinnamon

Directions:

1. In a blender, blend the coconut milk, peaches, honey, and cinnamon until smooth.
2. Pour the mixture into ice pop molds and freeze for about 5 hours.
3. Store in the freezer for up to a week with plastic wrap over the open tops of the molds.

Nutrition:

- **Calories:** 79;
- **Total fat:** 3 g;
- **Cholesterol:** 0 mg;
- **Fiber:** 2 g;
- **Protein:** 0 g;
- **Sodium:** 4 mg

70. MELON-LIME SORBET

Easy/Gluten-fee

Preparation time: 15 minutes plus 4 to 6 hours to freeze

Cooking time: 5 minutes

Servings: 8

Ingredients:

- 1 small honeydew melon, peeled, seeded, and cut into 1-inch chunks
- 1 small cantaloupe, peeled, seeded, and cut into 1-inch chunks
- 2 tablespoons honey
- 2 tablespoons freshly squeezed lime juice

- Pinch cinnamon
- Water as needed

Directions:

1. Spread the honeydew and cantaloupe out on a baking sheet lined with parchment paper and put it in the freezer for 4 to 6 hours until frozen.
2. In a food processor, add the frozen melon chunks and the honey, lime juice, and cinnamon.
3. Pulse until smooth, adding water (a tablespoon at a time) if needed to purée the melon.
4. Transfer the mixture to a resealable container and place it in the freezer until set, about 30 minutes.

Nutrition:

- **Calories:** 97;
- **Total fat:** 0 g;
- **Cholesterol:** 0 mg;
- **Fiber:** 2 g;
- **Protein:** 2 g;
- **Sodium:** 39 mg

71. **MANDARIN AMBROSIA**

Easy/Gluten-free

Preparation time: 5 minutes plus 3 hours to freeze

Cooking time: 5 minutes

Servings: 6

Ingredients:

- ½ cup coconut cream, chilled in the refrigerator overnight

- 3 cups vegan mini marshmallows
- 1 cup shredded unsweetened coconut
- 3 small tangerines, peeled and segmented
- ½ cup sour cream

Directions:

1. In a large bowl, beat the cold coconut cream until it forms stiff peaks.
2. Stir in the marshmallows, coconut, tangerine segments, and sour cream until well mixed.
3. Cover and chill in the refrigerator for 3 hours before serving.

Nutrition:

- **Calories:** 281;
- **Total fat:** 22 g;
- **Cholesterol:** 4 mg;
- **Fiber:** 2 g;
- **Protein:** 6 g;
- **Sodium:** 31 mg

72. COCONUT-QUINOA PUDDING

Easy/Gluten-free

Preparation time: 5 minutes

Cooking time: 20 minutes

Servings: 6

Ingredients:

- 2 cups almond milk
- 1½ cups quinoa
- 1 cup light coconut milk
- ½ cup maple syrup
- Pinch salt
- 1 teaspoon pure vanilla extract

Directions:

1. In a large saucepan heat the almond milk, quinoa, coconut milk, maple syrup, salt, and vanilla over medium-high heat.
2. Bring the quinoa mixture to a boil and then reduce the heat to low.
3. Simmer until the quinoa is tender, stirring frequently, about 20 minutes.
4. Remove the pudding from the heat.

Nutrition:

- **Calories:** 241;
- **Total fat:** 6 g;
- **Cholesterol:** 0 mg;
- **Fiber:** 2 g;
- **Protein:** 6 g;
- **Sodium:** 161 mg

73. GOAT CHEESE–STUFFED PEARS WITH HAZELNUTS

Easy/Gluten-free

Preparation time: 4 minutes

Cooking time: 5 minutes

Servings: 20

Ingredients:

- 1 tablespoon butter
- 2 ripe pears, cored and hollowed out with a spoon
- ½ cup of water
- 8 tablespoons goat cheese
- 2 tablespoons honey
- ¼ cup roughly chopped hazelnuts

Directions:

1. Preheat the oven to 350°F.
2. In a medium skillet, melt the butter over medium heat.
3. Place the pears in the skillet, skin-side up, and lightly brown them, about 2 minutes.
4. Place the pears in an 8-by-8-inch square baking dish, hollow side up, and pour the water into the baking dish, taking care not to get any in the hollow part of the pears.
5. Roast the pears until softened, about 10 minutes. Remove the pears from the oven.
6. In a small bowl, stir together the goat cheese, honey, and hazelnuts.
7. Evenly divide the goat cheese mixture between the pear halves and put them back in the oven for 5 minutes.
8. Serve warm.

Nutrition:

- **Calories:** 185;
- **Total fat:** 9 g;

- **Cholesterol:** 15 mg;
- **Fiber:** 2 g;
- **Protein:** 4 g;
- **Sodium:** 17 mg

74. BUTTERMILK PANNA COTTA WITH MANGO

Easy/Gluten-free

Preparation time: 10 minutes

Cooking time: 2 minutes

Servings: 4

Ingredients:

- ½ cup full-fat coconut milk
- 1½ teaspoons agar-agar
- 1½ cups buttermilk
- ¼ cup honey
- 2 cups roughly chopped fresh mango

Directions:

1. Pour the coconut milk into a small saucepan and sprinkle the agar-agar over it and let the coconut milk stand for 5 minutes.
2. Place the saucepan over medium-low heat and heat until the agar-agar is dissolved, about 2 minutes.
3. Add the buttermilk and honey and stir to combine.
4. Pour the panna cotta mixture into 4 (6-ounces) ramekins. Wrap them in plastic wrap and refrigerate them for about 3 hours, or until set.
5. Loosen the panna cotta by running a knife around the inside edges of the ramekins. Invert them onto serving plates.
6. Top with mango and serve.

Nutrition:

- **Calories:** 226;
- **Total fat:** 8 g;
- **Cholesterol:** 14 mg;
- **Fiber:** 2 g;
- **Protein:** 6 g;
- **Sodium:** 106 mg

75. <u>SWEET POTATO–CINNAMON PARFAITS</u>

Easy/Gluten-free

Preparation time: 15 minutes

Cooking time: 15 minutes

Servings: 4

Ingredients:

- 2 sweet potatoes, peeled and cut into ½-inch chunks
- 1 cup coconut cream, chilled in the refrigerator overnight
- ¼ cup maple syrup
- ¼ teaspoon ground cinnamon
- Pinch sea salt
- ½ cup roughly chopped hazelnuts

Directions:

1. Place the sweet potatoes in a large saucepan and fill the pan with water until the sweet potatoes are covered by about an inch. Bring to a boil over high heat and then reduce the heat and simmer until the sweet potatoes are tender but not mushy about 15 minutes. Drain and mash until smooth with a potato masher.

2. Transfer the sweet potatoes to a resealable container, and set it in the refrigerator until completely cooled about 2 hours.

3. In a large bowl, whip the cold coconut cream until stiff peaks form.

4. In a medium bowl, stir together the sweet potatoes, maple syrup, cinnamon, and salt until smooth.

5. Fold half the whipped coconut cream into the sweet potato mixture, keeping as much volume as possible.

6. Chill the sweet potato mixture in the refrigerator for 1 hour.

7. Spoon the sweet potato mixture into 4 bowls and divide the remaining whipped coconut cream between the bowls.

8. Top with hazelnuts before serving.

Nutrition:

- **Calories:** 281;
- **Total fat:** 12 g;
- **Cholesterol:** 0 mg;
- **Fiber:** 2 g;
- **Protein:** 2 g;
- **Sodium:** 70 mg

76. FLOURLESS DARK CHOCOLATE CAKE

Easy/Gluten-free

Preparation time: 10 minutes

Cooking time: 45 minutes

Servings: 12

Ingredients:

- ½ cup of water
- ¾ cup coconut sugar or granulated sugar
- ⅛ teaspoon of sea salt
- 1¼ pounds bittersweet chocolate (containing at least 60% cacao), roughly chopped
- 1 cup salted butter, cut into 1-inch cubes, plus more for greasing pan
- 7 eggs
- 2 teaspoons pure vanilla extract

Directions:

1. Preheat the oven to 300°F. Grease a 9-inch round springform pan and set the pan on a piece of foil. Fold the foil up the outside of the pan, forming a waterproof layer. Set aside.

2. In a small saucepan, combine the water, sugar, and salt over medium-high heat, stirring until the sugar is completely dissolved. Remove the pan from the heat and set aside.

3. Place the chocolate in a large bowl over a medium saucepan of simmering water and stir until the chocolate has melted.

4. Remove the chocolate from the heat and beat in the butter (one cube at a time) with a hand mixer on medium speed until well blended.

5. Beat in the sugar mixture and the eggs (one at a time) at medium speed. Add the vanilla and beat until smooth.

6. Pour the batter into the prepared springform pan and place the pan into a larger pan. Pour boiling water into the larger pan until it reaches one inch up the sides of the springform pan.

7. Bake the cake until the edges are firm, about 45 minutes. Remove the cake from the oven and let cool on a rack.

8. Chill the cake in the refrigerator overnight. Remove from the springform pan when ready to serve.

Nutrition:

- **Calories:** 416;
- **Total fat:** 30 g;
- **Cholesterol:** 116 mg;
- **Fiber:** 2 g;
- **Protein:** 2 g;
- **Sodium:** 186mg

Chapter 9. DESSERTS

77. BLUEBERRY-VANILLA CRUMBLE

Medium/Gluten-free

Preparation time: 10 minutes

Cooking time: 40 minutes

Servings: 12

Ingredients:

- ¾ cup coconut oil, plus more for coating the pan
- 1 cup whole-wheat flour
- 2 cups uncooked quick or rolled oats
- ½ cup tightly packed brown sugar
- ½ cup hemp hearts
- 1½ teaspoons lemon zest
- 1 teaspoon ground cinnamon
- ½ teaspoon ground nutmeg
- ½ teaspoon salt
- 1 teaspoon vanilla extract
- 3½ cups fresh blueberries, rinsed

Directions:

1. Preheat the oven to 375°F. Line a 9-inch square baking pan with parchment paper or coat with coconut oil.

2. In a large mixing bowl, combine the flour, oats, sugar, hemp hearts, lemon zest, cinnamon, nutmeg, salt, coconut oil, and vanilla.

3. Use clean, dry hands to combine all ingredients, working the mixture between your fingers until a crumbly texture form. Divide in half, spreading one half in the prepared baking pan. Press firmly into the bottom of the pan to create an even crust.

4. Arrange the fresh blueberries in a single layer on top of the crust. Top with the remaining crumb mixture, breaking up large chunks and distributing evenly. Gently press to pack the mixture loosely.

5. Bake for 35 to 40 minutes, or until the top layer becomes golden brown and the blueberries start to bubble through the top layer. Remove from the oven and allow to cool for 5 to 10 minutes before serving.

Nutrition:

- **Calories:** 300;

- **Total fat:** 18 g;
- **Cholesterol:** 0 mg;
- **Fiber:** 2 g;
- **Protein:** 6 g;
- **Sodium:** 100 mg

---

78. GRILLED PEACHES WITH CARDAMOM WHIPPED CREAM

Easy/Gluten-free

Preparation time: 10 minutes

Cooking time: 5 minutes

Servings: 4

Ingredients:

- ½ cup heavy (whipping) cream
- 1 tablespoon brown sugar
- ½ teaspoon vanilla extract
- ¼ teaspoon ground cardamom
- 4 ripe peaches, halved and pitted
- 1 tablespoon canola or grapeseed oil
- 1½ tablespoons honey, for drizzling

Directions:

1. Use a hand or stand mixer to whip the heavy cream. Add the sugar, vanilla, and cardamom, and beat on high speed until peaks form. Chill in the refrigerator until needed.
2. Heat your grill or stove-top grill pan to medium heat. Brush the peach halves with oil to prevent sticking, then place flat-side down to sear. Grill for 4 minutes, or until grill marks form, then remove and place two halves in each serving bowl. Drizzle with the honey.
3. Remove the whipped cream from the fridge and divide it evenly among the bowls. Serve immediately.

Nutrition:

- **Calories:** 230;
- **Total fat:** 15 g;
- **Cholesterol:** 40 mg;
- **Fiber:** 2 g;
- **Protein:** 2 g;
- **Sodium:** 15 mg

79. DELICIOUS BROWNIES

Easy/Dairy-free

Preparation time: 10 minutes

Cooking time: 25 minutes

Servings: 4

Ingredients:

- 5 ounces of chocolate 86% (sugarless); melted
- 4 tablespoons of ghee, melted
- 3 eggs
- ½ cup of Swerve
- ¼ cup of mascarpone cheese
- ¼ cup of cocoa powder

Directions:

1. Take a big bowl; combine the melted chocolate with the ghee, eggs, swerve, cheese and cocoa. Whisk well, pour into a cake pan, introduce in the oven and cook at 375 degrees F for 25 minutes.
2. Cut into medium brownies and serve.

Nutrition:

- **Calories:** 120
- **Total Carbohydrate:** 9 g
- **Cholesterol:** 43 mg
- **Total Fat:** 27 g
- **Fiber:** 6 g
- **Protein:** 20 g

80. ICE CREAM WITH AVOCADO

Medium/Dairy-free

Preparation time: 10 minutes

Cooking time: 30 minutes

Servings: 6

Ingredients:

- 1 peeled and pitted the avocado
- 1½ teaspoon of vanilla paste
- 1 cup of coconut milk
- 2 tablespoons of almond butter

- Drops of stevia
- ¼ teaspoon of Ceylon cinnamon

Directions:

1. Combine all ingredients in a food blender. Blend until smooth. Transfer the mixture into Popsicle molds and insert popsicle sticks. Freeze for 4 hours or until firm. Serve.

Nutrition
- **Calories:** 268
- **Total Carbohydrate:** 9 g
- **Cholesterol:** 42 mg
- **Total Fat:** 20 g
- **Fiber:** 4 g
- **Protein:** 15 g

81. CHOCOLATE CAKE WITH BLUEBERRY

Medium/Gluten-free

Preparation time: 10 minutes

Cooking time: 40 minutes

Servings: 8

Ingredients:

- 2 eggs, stripped into whites and yolks
- 25 g of cocoa powder
- 50 g of almond flour
- 20 g of flax flour
- 1 teaspoon of sweetener (or to taste)
- 150 g of sour cream
- 50 g of vegetable oil
- 2 teaspoon of baking powder

- Vanilla or vanilla extract to taste

Directions:

1. Turn on the oven to 180 degrees.
2. Beat the squirrel to stable foam.
3. Beat yolks with sweetener.
4. Add sour cream and vegetable oil and mix.
5. Add all the dry ingredients and mix again, you can use a mixer.
6. Add proteins in two steps and mix them gently into the dough.
7. Use the form 16 cm in diameter.
8. Put in the oven for 25 minutes.
9. Cut the cake into two. You can soak them with a mixture of 1 tablespoon. of water and 1 teaspoon of Liquor.

Nutrition:

- **Calories:** 295
- **Total Carbohydrate:** 9 g
- **Cholesterol:** 52 mg
- **Total Fat:** 27 g
- **Fiber:** 2 g
- **Protein:** 9 g

82. COCONUT RASPBERRY CAKE

Easy/Gluten-free

Preparation time: 1 hour and 10 minutes

Cooking time: 10 Minutes.

Servings: 6

Ingredients:

FOR THE BISCUIT:

- 2 cups almond flour
- 1 egg
- 1 tablespoon of ghee, melted
- ½ teaspoon of baking soda

FOR THE COCONUT LAYER:

- 1 cup of coconut milk
- ¼ cup of coconut oil, melted

- 3 cups coconut, shredded
- 1/3 cup of stevia
- 5 grams of food gelatin

FOR THE RASPBERRY LAYER:

- 1 cup of raspberries
- 1 teaspoon of stevia
- 3 tablespoons of chia seeds
- 5 grams of food gelatin

Directions:

1. In a bowl, combine the almond flour with the eggs, ghee, and baking soda; stir well. Press on the bottom of the springform pan, and introduce in the oven at 350 degrees F for 15 minutes. Leave aside to cool down.
2. Meanwhile, in a pan, combine the raspberries with 1-teaspoon stevia, chia seeds, and gelatin; stir, and cook for 5 minutes. Take off the heat, cool down, and spread over the biscuit layer.
3. In another small pan, combine the coconut milk with the coconut, oil, gelatin, 1/3 cup stevia; stir for 1-2 minutes. Take off the heat, cool down, and spread over the coconut milk.
4. Cool the cake in the fridge for 1 hour, slice, and serve.

Nutrition:

- **Calories:** 221
- **Total Carbohydrate:** 9 g
- **Cholesterol:** 32 mg
- **Total Fat:** 12 g
- **Fiber:** 2 g
- **Protein:** 7 g

83. CHOCOLATE MOUSSE

Easy/Gluten-free

Preparation time: 5 minutes

Cooking time: 5 minutes

Servings: 4

Ingredients:

- 1 tablespoon. of cocoa powder
- 2 oz. of cream cheese
- 2 oz. of butter

- 3 oz. of heavy whipping cream
- Stevia to taste

Directions:

1. Melt the butter a bit and mix with the sweetener. Stir until blended.
2. Add the cream cheese and cocoa powder and blend until smooth.
3. Carefully whip heavy cream and gradually add to the mixture.
4. Refrigerate it for 30 minutes.

Nutrition:

- **Calories:** 227
- **Total Carbohydrate:** 8 g
- **Cholesterol:** 42 mg
- **Total Fat:** 36 g
- **Fiber:** 2 g
- **Protein:** 4 g

84. SWEET GREEN COOKIES

Medium/Gluten-free

Preparation time: 10 minutes

Cooking time: 30 minutes

Servings: 12 cookies, 3 per serving

Ingredients:

- 165 g green peas
- 80 g chopped Medjool dates
- 60 g silken tofu, mashed
- 100 g almond flour
- 1 teaspoon baking powder
- 12 almonds

Directions:

1. Preheat oven to 180º C/350 º F.
2. Combine peas and dates in a food processor.
3. Process until the thick paste is formed.
4. Transfer the pea mixture into a bowl. Stir in tofu, almond flour, and baking powder.
5. Shape the mixture into 12 balls.
6. Arrange balls onto the baking sheet, lined with parchment paper. Flatten each ball with oiled palm.

7. Insert an almond into each cookie. Bake the cookies for twenty-five to thirty minutes or until gently golden.

8. Cool on a wire rack before serving.

Nutrition:

- **Calories:** 221
- **Total Fat:** 10.3 g
- **Total Carbohydrate:** 26.2 g
- **Dietary Fiber:** 6 g
- **Total Sugars:** 15.1 g
- **Protein:** 8.2 g

85. CHICKPEA CHOCO SLICES

Easy/Gluten-free

Preparation time: 10 minutes

Cooking time: 50 minutes

Servings: 12 slices, 2 per serving

Ingredients:

- 400 g can chickpeas,
- Rinsed, drained 250g almond butter
- 70 ml maple syrup
- 15 ml vanilla paste
- 1 pinch salt
- 2 g baking powder
- 2 g baking soda
- 40 g vegan chocolate chips

Directions:

1. Preheat oven to 180º C/350º F.
2. Grease large baking pan with coconut oil.
3. Combine chickpeas, almond butter, maple syrup, vanilla, salt, baking powder, and baking soda in a food blender.
4. Blend until smooth. Stir in half the chocolate chips.
5. Spread the batter into the prepared baking pan.
6. Sprinkle with reserved chocolate chips.
7. Bake for 45-50 minutes or until an inserted toothpick comes out neat.

8. Appease on a wire rack for twenty minutes. slice and serve.

Nutrition:

- **Calories:** 426
- **Total Fat:** 27.2 g
- **Total Carbohydrate:** 39.2 g
- **Dietary Fiber:** 4.9 g
- **Total Sugars:** 15.7 g
- **Protein:** 10 g

86. HOMEMADE LEMON CURD

Easy/Gluten-free

Preparation time: 10 minutes

Cooking time: 5 minutes

Servings: 8

Ingredients:

- 1 large egg
- 3 large egg yolks
- ½ cup of sugar
- ⅓ cup freshly squeezed lemon juice
- 2 tablespoons unsalted butter
- Pinch salt
- 1½ tablespoons heavy (whipping) cream

Directions:

1. In a small saucepan, whisk the egg, egg yolks, and sugar together. Once combined, turn the burner to low heat and whisk in the lemon juice, butter, and salt.

2. Slowly heat until the butter melts and the mixture start to thicken. Heat to 170° F (about 5 minutes), and verify using a kitchen thermometer. Remove from the heat, stir in the cream, and transfer to a mason jar. Cover and chill for at least 2 hours before serving to allow the curd to set.

Nutrition:

- **Calories:** 161;
- **Total fat:** 6 g;
- **Cholesterol:** 45 mg;
- **Fiber:** 2 g;
- **Protein:** 2 g;

- **Sodium**: 178 mg

87. EASY MANGO SORBET

Easy/Gluten-free

Preparation time: 10 minutes

Cooking time: 2 minutes

Servings: 4

Ingredients:

- ½ cup of coconut milk
- ½ cup of sugar
- 1 (12-ounces) bag frozen mango chunks
- 1 tablespoon freshly squeezed lime juice
- Fresh mint or basil, for garnish (optional)

Directions:

1. In a small saucepan over low heat, make a syrup by heating the coconut milk. Add the sugar and let it dissolve completely, stirring often about 2 minutes.

2. Add the syrup to a blender along with the frozen mango and lime juice. Blend until smooth, then transfer to a loaf pan or baking dish. Cover and place in the freezer for 2 to 4 hours, or until ready to serve. With an ice cream scoop or tablespoon, scoop out the sorbet into four small bowls. Top with the mint or basil before serving, if desired.

Nutrition:

- **Calories:** 210;
- **Total fat:** 6 g;
- **Cholesterol:** 0 mg;
- **Fiber:** 2 g;
- **Protein:** 1 g;
- **Sodium:** 0 mg

88. CHICKPEA COOKIE DOUGH

Easy/Gluten-free

Preparation time: 10 minutes

Cooking time: 0 minutes

Servings: 4

Ingredients:

- 400 g can chickpeas, rinsed, drained

- 130 g smooth peanut butter
- 10 ml vanilla extract
- ½ teaspoon cinnamon
- 10 g chia seeds
- 40 g quality dark Vegan chocolate chips

Direction:

1. Drain chickpeas in a colander.
2. Remove the skin from the chickpeas.
3. Place chickpeas, peanut butter, vanilla, cinnamon, and chia in a food blender.
4. Blend until smooth.
5. Stir in chocolate chips and divide among four serving bowls.
6. Serve.

Nutrition:

- **Calories:** 376
- **Total Fat:** 20.9 g
- **Total Carbohydrate:** 37.2 g
- **Dietary Fiber:** 7.3 g
- **Total Sugars:** 3.3 g
- **Protein:** 14.2 g

89. BANANA BARS

Medium/Dairy-free

Preparation time: 10 minutes

Cooking time: 30 minutes

Servings: 8

Ingredients:

- 130 g smooth peanut butter
- 60 ml maple syrup
- 1 banana, mashed
- 45 ml water
- 15 g ground flax seeds
- 95 g cooked quinoa
- 25 g chia seeds
- 5 ml vanilla

- 90 g quick-cooking oats
- 55 g whole-wheat flour
- 5 g baking powder
- 5 g cinnamon
- 1 pinch salt

TOPPING:

- 5 ml melted coconut oil
- 30 g vegan chocolate, chopped

Directions:

1. Preheat oven to 180° C/35 ° F.
2. Line 16 cm baking dish with parchment paper.
3. Put together water and flax seeds in a small bowl. Place aside 10 minutes.
4. In a separate bowl, combine peanut butter, maple syrup, and banana. Fold in the flax seed's mixture.
5. Once you have a smooth mixture, stir in quinoa, chia seeds, vanilla extract, oat, whole-wheat flour, baking powder, cinnamon, and salt.
6. Pour the batter into a prepared baking dish. Cut into 8 bars.
7. Bake the bars for 30 minutes.
8. In the meantime, make the topping; combine chocolate and coconut oil in a heatproof bowl. Set over simmering water, until melted.
9. Remove the bars from the oven. Place on a wire rack for 15 minutes to cool.
10. Remove the bars from the baking dish, and drizzle with chocolate topping.
11. Serve.

Nutrition:

- **Calories:** 278
- **Total Fat:** 11.9 g
- **Total Carbohydrate:** 35.5 g
- **Dietary Fiber:** 5.8 g
- **Total Sugars:** 10.8 g
- **Protein:** 9.4 g

90. **PROTEIN DONUTS**

Easy/Dairy-free

Preparation Time: 5 minutes

Cooking Time: 20 minutes

Servings: 10 donuts, 2 per serving

Ingredients:

- 85 g coconut flour
- 110 g vanilla-flavored germinated brown rice protein powder
- 25 g almond flour
- 50 g maple sugar
- 30 ml melted coconut oil
- 8 g baking powder
- 115 ml soy milk
- ½ teaspoon apple cider vinegar
- ½ teaspoon vanilla paste
- ½ teaspoon cinnamon
- 30 ml organic applesauce

ADDITIONAL:

- 30 g powdered coconut sugar
- 10 g cinnamon

Directions:

1. Add all the dried ingredients in a large cup.
2. In a separate bowl, whisk the milk with applesauce, coconut oil, and cider vinegar.
3. Fold the wet ingredients into dry and stir until blended thoroughly.
4. Heat oven to 180C/350F and grease 10-hole donut pan.
5. Spoon the prepared batter into a greased donut pan.
6. Bake the donuts for 15-20 minutes.
7. Sprinkle with coconut sugar and cinnamon while the donuts are still warm,
8. Serve warm.

Nutrition:

- **Calories:** 270
- **Total Fat:** 9.3 g
- **Total Carbohydrate:** 28.4g
- **Dietary Fiber:** 10.2 g
- **Total Sugars:** 10.1 g
- **Prote**in: 20.5 g

91. LENTIL BALLS

Easy/Gluten-free

Preparation time: 10 minutes

Cooking time: 0 minutes

Servings: 16 balls, 2 per serving

Ingredients:

- 150 g cooked green lentils
- 10 ml coconut oil
- 5 g coconut sugar
- 180 g quick-cooking oats
- 40 g unsweetened coconut, shredded
- 40 g raw pumpkin seeds
- 110 g peanut butter
- 40 ml maple syrup

Directions:

1. Add all ingredients in a large bowl, as listed.
2. Shape the mixture into 16 balls.
3. Arrange the balls onto a plate, lined with parchment paper.
4. Refrigerate 30 minutes.
5. Serve.

Nutrition:

- **Calories:** 305
- **Total Fat:** 13.7 g
- **Total Carbohydrate:** 35.4 g
- **Dietary Fiber:** 9.5 g
- **Total Sugars:** 6.3 g
- **Protein:** 12.6 g

92. HOMEMADE GRANOLA

Easy/Gluten-free

Preparation time: 10 minutes

Cooking time: 24 minutes

Servings: 8

Ingredients:

- 270 g rolled oats
- 100 g coconut flakes
- 40 g pumpkin seeds
- 80 g hemp seeds
- 30 ml coconut oil
- 70 ml maple syrup
- 50 g Goji berries

Direction:

1. Add all ingredients on a large baking sheet.
2. Preheat oven to 180C°/350º F.
3. Bake the granola for 12 minutes. Remove from the oven and stir.
4. Bake an additional 12 minutes.
5. Serve at room temperature.

Nutrition:

- **Calories:** 344
- **Total Fat:** 17.4 g
- **Total Carbohydrate:** 39.7 g
- **Dietary Fiber:** 5.8 g
- **Total Sugars:** 12.9 g
- **Protein:** 9.9 g

93. <u>COOKIE ALMOND BALLS</u>

Easy/Gluten-free

Preparation time: 15 minutes

Cooking time: 0 minutes

Servings: 16 balls, 2 per serving

Ingredients:

- 100 g almond meal
- 60 g vanilla-flavored rice protein powder
- 80 g almond butter or any nut butter
- 10 drops Stevia
- 15 ml coconut oil
- 15 g coconut cream
- 40 g vegan chocolate chips

Directions:

1. Combine almond meal and protein powder in a large bowl.
2. Fold in almond butter, Stevia, coconut oil, and coconut cream.
3. If the mixture is too crumbly, add some water. Fold in chopped chocolate and stir until combined.
4. Shape the mixture into 16 balls.
5. You can additionally roll the balls into almond flour.
6. Serve.

Nutrition:

- **Calories:** 132
- **Total Fat:** 8.4 g
- **Total Carbohydrate:** 6.7 g
- **Dietary Fiber:** 2.2 g
- **Total Sugars:** 3.1 g
- **Protein:** 8.1 g

94. <u>SPICED DUTCH COOKIES</u>

Easy/Dairy-free

Preparation time: 20 minutes

Cooking time: 8 minutes

Servings: 6

Ingredients:

- 180 g almond flour
- 55 ml coconut oil, melted
- 60 g rice protein powder, vanilla flavor

- 1 banana, mashed 40g Chia seeds
- Spice mix: 15g allspice
- 1 pinch white pepper
- 1 pinch ground coriander seeds
- 1 pinch ground mace

Directions:

1. Preheat oven to 190º C/375º F.
2. Soak chia seeds in ½ cup water. Place aside 10 minutes.
3. Mash banana in a large bowl.
4. Fold in almond flour, coconut oil, protein powder, and spice mix.
5. Add soaked chia seeds and stir to combine.
6. Stir until the dough is combined and soft. If needed add 1-2 tablespoons water.
7. Roll the dough to 1cm thick. Cut out cookies.
8. Arrange the cookies onto the baking sheet, lined with parchment paper.
9. Bake 7-8 minutes.
10. Serve at room temperature.

Nutrition:

- **Calories:** 278
- **Total Fat:** 20 g
- **Total Carbohydrate:** 13.1 g
- **Dietary Fiber:** 5.9 g
- **Total Sugars:** 2.4 g
- **Protein:** 13.1 g

95. STONE FRUIT FOIL PACKETS WITH VANILLA ICE CREAM

Easy/Gluten-free

Preparation time: 10 minutes

Cooking time: 10 minutes

Servings: 4

Ingredients:

- Nonstick cooking spray
- 2 large nectarines, halved and pitted
- 4 plums, halved and pitted
- 2 tablespoons loosely packed brown sugar

- 1 tablespoon lemon zest
- Dash ground cinnamon
- 12 Nilla Wafers, crushed
- 3 cups vanilla ice cream (¾ cup per serving)

Directions:

1. Preheat the oven to 350° F if not using a grill.
2. Prepare four foil packs by stacking two layers of aluminum foil, leaving plenty of room to fold and seal around the contents.
3. Lightly coat with nonstick cooking spray, then arrange one nectarine half and two plum halves in the center of each. Sprinkle one-quarter of the brown sugar, lemon zest, and cinnamon over each, then fold the edges of the foil up and over the contents, folding and pinching the edges to seal.
4. Place on the grill over medium heat or bake for 10 minutes. Remove from the heat and carefully vent the foil packs, taking care to keep your fingers and faces away from the released steam.
5. Top the contents of each foil pack with the crushed wafers and vanilla ice cream and serve immediately.

Nutrition:

- **Calories:** 351;
- **Total fat:** 14 g;
- **Cholesterol:** 45 mg;
- **Fiber:** 2 g;
- **Protein:** 5 g;
- **Sodium:** 125 mg

96. LAYERED KEY LIME CUPS

Easy/Gluten-free

Preparation time: 10 minutes

Cooking time: 2 minutes

Servings: 4

Ingredients:

- 2 avocados, peeled and pitted
- 1 very ripe banana, peeled
- ¼ cup freshly squeezed key lime juice
- 1 tablespoon key lime zest, plus more for garnish
- ¼ cup maple syrup
- 1 teaspoon vanilla extract

- 2 pinches salt, divided
- ¼ cup Medjool dates pitted and softened in warm water
- ¼ cup macadamia nuts, finely chopped, plus more for garnish
- ½ cup unsweetened coconut flakes
- 1 container (5.3-ounces) vanilla, low-fat Greek yogurt

Directions:

1. In a blender, combine the avocado with the banana, key lime juice, key lime zest, maple syrup, vanilla, and 1 pinch of salt. Blend until a smooth, creamy texture forms.

2. Remove the dates from the water and pat dry. Add to the bowl of a food processor along with the macadamia nuts, coconut flakes, and the remaining pinch of salt for the crust. Process until a crumbly mixture form.

3. Prepare four single-serving ramekins or low tumblers. Add the crust mixture to the bottom of each and gently pack down. Divide the avocado mixture evenly among them, then top each with a dollop of vanilla yogurt. Garnish with additional nuts or lime zest, if desired, and serve.

Nutrition:

- **Calories:** 390;
- **Total fat:** 22 g;
- **Cholesterol:** 0 mg;
- **Fiber:** 2 g;
- **Protein:** 5 g;
- **Sodium:** 210 mg

97. LEMON CURD & RASPBERRY S'MORES

Easy/Dairy-free

Preparation time: 5 minutes

Cooking time: 5 minutes

Servings: 4

Ingredients:

- 4 graham crackers
- 2 tablespoons Homemade Lemon Curd
- 2 tablespoons raspberry jam or jelly
- 4 white chocolate squares
- 4 jumbo marshmallows

Directions:

1. To make each some more, break a graham cracker in half to form two squares. Spread the lemon curd onto one half and the raspberry jam or jelly on the other half. Place the white chocolate square on one half.

2. Toast the marshmallows over a grill, campfire, or stove-top burner. Once heated, place on top of the white chocolate square and top the some more with the other half of the graham cracker. Serve immediately.

Nutrition:

- **Calories:** 311;
- **Total fat:** 8 g;
- **Cholesterol:** 45 mg;
- **Fiber:** 2 g;
- **Protein:** 12 g;
- **Sodium:** 217 mg

98. CARROT CAKE COOKIES WITH TOASTED PECANS

Easy/Gluten-free

Preparation time: 10 minutes

Cooking time: 15 minutes

Servings: 18

Ingredients:

- Nonstick cooking spray
- ½ cup butter softened
- ¾ cup granulated sugar
- ¾ cup tightly packed brown sugar
- 1 large egg
- ½ teaspoon vanilla extract
- ¾ cup all-purpose flour
- ¾ cup whole-wheat flour
- 1 teaspoon ground cinnamon
- ½ teaspoon baking soda
- ½ teaspoon baking powder
- ¼ teaspoon salt
- 1 cup shredded carrots

- 1 cup chopped pecans, toasted
- ½ cup raisins

Directions:

1. Preheat the oven to 375°F. Prepare a baking sheet with nonstick cooking spray or parchment paper.
2. In a large bowl, cream the butter, granulated sugar, and brown sugar together until fluffy. Add the egg and vanilla, and stir to combine.
3. In another large bowl, combine the all-purpose flour, whole-wheat flour, cinnamon, baking soda, baking powder, salt, carrots, pecans, and raisins, then add to the wet ingredients. Fold together to form a thick batter.
4. Spoon the batter onto the prepared baking sheet, leaving about 1½ inches between each. Use a second baking sheet if needed. Bake for 12 to 14 minutes, or until the cookies are golden brown. Serve when they are cool enough if you can wait that long.

Nutrition:

- **Calories:** 190;
- **Total fat:** 10 g;
- **Cholesterol:** 25 mg;
- **Fiber:** 2 g;
- **Protein:** 2 g;
- **Sodium:** 117 mg

99. <u>CHIPOTLE-CHOCOLATE CHIA PUDDING</u>

Easy/Gluten-free

Preparation time: 5 minutes

Cooking time: 2 minutes

Servings: 2

Ingredients:

- ½ cup chia seeds
- 1 cup 2% chocolate milk
- 1 teaspoon cocoa powder, unsweetened
- ½ teaspoon ground cinnamon
- ½ teaspoon vanilla extract
- ¼ teaspoon ground nutmeg
- Pinch chipotle chili powder

- ½ tablespoon maple syrup or honey
- Pinch salt

Directions:

1. In a small bowl, cover the chia seeds with chocolate milk. Stir, then cover and refrigerate for at least 1 hour.

2. Remove from the refrigerator and transfer to a blender. Add the cocoa powder, cinnamon, vanilla, nutmeg, chili powder, maple syrup, and salt, and blend on high speed until a smooth texture form. Use a spatula to scrape down the walls of the blender as needed.

3. Spoon into two bowls, and serve or store in the refrigerator for up to 3 days.

Nutrition:
- **Calories:** 351;
- **Total fat:** 17 g;
- **Cholesterol:** 34 mg;
- **Fiber:** 2 g;
- **Protein:** 12 g
- **Sodium:** 150 mg

Chapter 10. SNACKS AND COOKIES

100.   GRILLED SALMON BURGER

Easy/Gluten-free

Preparation Time: 15 minutes

Cooking time: 10 minutes

Servings: 4

Ingredients:

- 16 ounces (450 g) pink salmon fillet, minced
- 1 cup (250 g) prepared mashed potatoes
- 1 shallot (about 40 g), chopped
- 1 large egg (about 60 g), lightly beaten
- 2 tablespoons (7 g) fresh coriander, chopped
- 4 Hamburger buns (about 60 g each), split
- 1 large tomato (about 150 g), sliced
- 8 (15 g) Romaine lettuce leaves
- 1/4 cup (60 g) mayonnaise
- Salt and freshly ground black pepper
- Cooking oil spray

Directions:

1. Combine the salmon, mashed potatoes, shallot, egg, and coriander in a mixing bowl. Season with salt and pepper.
2. Spoon about 2 tablespoons of mixture and form into patties.
3. Preheat your grill or griddle on high. Grease with cooking oil spray.
4. Grill the salmon patties for 4-5 minutes on each side or until cooked through. Transfer to a clean plate and cover to keep warm.
5. Spread some mayonnaise on the bottom half of the buns. Top with lettuce, salmon patty, and tomato. Cover with bun tops.
6. Serve and enjoy.

Nutrition:

- **Calories:** 395
- **Fat:** 18.0 g
- **Carbohydrates:** 38.8 g
- **Protein:** 21.8 g

- **Sodium:** 383 mg

101. EASY SALMON BURGER

Easy/Gluten-free

Preparation Time: 15 minutes

Cooking time: 15 minutes

Servings: 6

Ingredients:

- 16 ounces (450 g) pink salmon, minced
- 1 cup (250 g) prepared mashed potatoes
- 1 medium (110 g) onion, chopped
- 1 stalk celery (about 60 g), finely chopped
- 1 large egg (about 60 g), lightly beaten
- 2 tablespoons (7 g) fresh cilantro, chopped
- 1 cup (100 g) breadcrumbs
- Vegetable oil, for deep frying
- Salt and freshly ground black pepper

Directions:

1. Combine the salmon, mashed potatoes, onion, celery, egg, and cilantro in a mixing bowl. Season to taste and mix thoroughly. Spoon about 2 Tablespoon mixture, roll in breadcrumbs, and then form into small patties.
2. Heat oil in a non-stick frying pan. Cook your salmon patties for 5 minutes on each side or until golden brown and crispy.
3. Serve in burger buns and with coleslaw on the side if desired.
4. Enjoy.

Nutrition:

- **Calories:** 230
- **Fat:** 7.9 g
- **Carbs:** 20.9 g
- **Protein:** 18.9 g
- **Sodium:** 298 mg

102. SALMON SANDWICH WITH AVOCADO AND EGG

Easy/Gluten-free/Vegan

Preparation Time: 15 minutes

Cooking time: 10 minutes

Servings: 4

Ingredients:

- 8 ounces (250 g) smoked salmon, thinly sliced
- 1 medium (200 g) ripe avocado, thinly sliced
- 4 large poached eggs (about 60 g each)
- 4 slices whole-wheat bread (about 30 g each)
- 2 cups (60 g) arugula or baby rocket
- Salt and freshly ground black pepper

Directions:

1. Place 1 bread slice on a plate top with arugula, avocado, salmon, and poached egg. Season with salt and pepper. Repeat procedure for the remaining ingredients.
2. Serve and enjoy.

Nutrition:

- **Calories:** 310
- **Fat:** 18.2 g
- **Carbohydrates:** 16.4 g
- **Protein:** 21.3 g
- **Sodium:** 383 mg

103.   SALMON SPINACH AND COTTAGE CHEESE SANDWICH

Easy/Gluten-free/Vegan

Preparation Time: 15 minutes

Cooking time: 10 minutes

Servings: 4

Ingredients:

- 4 ounces (125 g) cottage cheese
- 1/4 cup (15 g) chives, chopped
- 1 teaspoon (5 g) capers
- 1/2 teaspoon (2.5 g) grated lemon rind
- 4 (2 oz. or 60 g) smoked salmon
- 2 cups (60 g) loose baby spinach
- 1 medium (110 g) red onion, sliced thinly
- 8 slices rye bread (about 30 g each)
- Kosher salt and freshly ground black pepper

Directions:

1. Preheat your griddle or Panini press.
2. Mix together cottage cheese, chives, capers, and lemon rind in a small bowl.
3. Spread and divide the cheese mixture on 4 bread slices. Top with spinach, onion slices, and smoked salmon.
4. Cover with remaining bread slices.
5. Grill the sandwiches until golden and grill marks form on both sides.
6. Transfer to a serving dish.
7. Serve and enjoy.

Nutrition:

- **Calories:** 261
- **Fat:** 9.9 g
- **Carbohydrates:** 22.9 g
- **Protein:** 19.9 g
- **Sodium:** 1226 mg

104.   SALMON FETA AND PESTO WRAP

Easy/Dairy-free/Vegan

Preparation Time: 15 minutes

Cooking time: 10 minutes

Servings: 4

Ingredients:

- 8 ounces (250 g) smoked salmon fillet, thinly sliced

- 1 cup (150 g) feta cheese
- 8 (15 g) Romaine lettuce leaves
- 4 (6-inches) pita bread
- 1/4 cup (60 g) basil pesto sauce

Directions:

1. Place 1 pita bread on a plate. Top with lettuce, salmon, feta cheese, and pesto sauce. Fold or roll to enclose filling. Repeat procedure for the remaining ingredients.
2. Serve and enjoy.

Nutrition:

- **Calories:** 379
- **Fat:** 17.7 g
- **Carbohydrates:** 36.6 g
- **Protein:** 18.4 g
- **Sodium:** 554 mg

105.   SALMON CREAM CHEESE AND ONION ON BAGEL

Easy/Gluten-free/Vegan

Preparation Time: 15 minutes

Cooking time: 10 minutes

Servings: 4

Ingredients:

- 8 ounces (250 g) smoked salmon fillet, thinly sliced
- 1/2 cup (125 g) cream cheese
- 1 medium (110 g) onion, thinly sliced
- 4 bagels (about 80g each), split
- 2 tablespoons (7 g) fresh parsley, chopped
- Freshly ground black pepper, to taste

Directions:

1. Spread the cream cheese on each bottom's half of the bagels. Top with salmon and onion, season with pepper, sprinkle with parsley and then cover with bagel tops.
2. Serve and enjoy.

Nutrition:

- **Calories:** 309
- **Fat:** 14.1 g

- **Carbohydrates:** 32.0 g
- **Protein:** 14.7 g
- **Sodium:** 571 mg

106.   <u>**GREEK BAKLAVA**</u>

Medium/Dairy-free

Preparation time: 20 minutes

Cooking time: 20 minutes

Servings: 18

Ingredients:

- 1 (16 oz.) package phyllo dough
- 1 lb. chopped nuts
- 1 cup butter
- 1 teaspoon ground cinnamon
- 1 cup of water
- 1 cup white sugar
- 1 teaspoon. vanilla extract
- 1/2 cup honey

Directions:

1. Preheat the oven to 175° C or 350° Fahrenheit. Spread butter on the sides and bottom of a 9-in by the 13-in pan.

2. Chop the nuts then mix with cinnamon; set it aside. Unfurl the phyllo dough then halve the whole stack to fit the pan. Use a damp cloth to cover the phyllo to prevent drying as you proceed. Put two phyllo sheets in the pan then butter well. Repeat to make eight layered phyllo sheets. Scatter 2-3 tablespoons. nut mixture over the sheets then place two more phyllo sheets on top, butter then sprinkles with nuts. Layer as you go. The final layer should be six to eight phyllo sheets deep.

3. Make square or diamond shapes with a sharp knife up to the bottom of the pan. You can slice into four long rows for diagonal shapes. Bake until crisp and golden for 50 minutes.

4. Meanwhile, boil water and sugar until the sugar melts to make the sauce; mix in honey and vanilla. Let it simmer for 20 minutes.

5. Take the baklava out of the oven then drizzle with sauce right away; cool. Serve the baklava in cupcake papers. You can also freeze them without cover. The baklava will turn soggy when wrapped.

Nutrition:

- **Calories**: 393

- **Total Carbohydrate:** 37.5 g
- **Cholesterol:** 27 mg
- **Total Fat:** 25.9 g
- **Protein:** 6.1 g
- **Sodium:** 196 mg

107. GLAZED BANANAS IN PHYLLO NUT CUPS

Easy/Gluten-free

Preparation time: 30 minutes

Cooking time: 45 minutes

Servings: 6 servings.

Ingredients:

- 3/4 cup shelled pistachios
- 1/2 cup sugar
- 1 teaspoon. ground cinnamon
- 4 sheets phyllo dough, (14 inches' x 9 inches)
- 1/4 cup butter, melted

SAUCE:

- 3/4 cup butter, cubed
- 3/4 cup packed brown sugar
- 3 medium firm bananas, sliced
- 1/4 teaspoon. ground cinnamon
- 3 to 4 cups of vanilla ice cream

Directions:

1. Finely chop sugar and pistachios in a food processor; move to a bowl then mix in cinnamon. Slice each phyllo sheet to 6 four-inch squares, get rid of the trimmings. Pile the squares then use plastic wrap to cover.

2. Slather melted butter on each square one at a time then scatter a heaping tablespoonful of pistachio mixture. Pile 3 squares, flip each at an angle to misalign the corners. Force each stack on the sides and bottom of an oiled eight-oz. custard cup. Bake for 15-20 minutes in a 350 degrees F oven until golden; cool for 5 minutes. Move to a wire rack to completely cool.

3. Melt and boil brown sugar and butter in a saucepan to make the sauce; lower heat. Mix in cinnamon and bananas gently; heat completely. Put ice cream in the phyllo cups until full then put banana sauce on top. Serve right away.

Nutrition:

- **Calories:** 735
- **Total Carbohydrate:** 82 g
- **Cholesterol:** 111 mg
- **Total Fat:** 45 g
- **Fiber:** 3 g
- **Protein:** 7 g
- **Sodium:** 468 mg

108.   SALMON APPLE SALAD SANDWICH

Easy/Gluten-free/Vegan

Preparation Time: 15 minutes

Cooking Time: 10 minutes

Servings: 4

Ingredients:

- 4 ounces (125 g) canned pink salmon, drained and flaked
- 1 medium (180 g) red apple, cored and diced
- 1 celery stalk (about 60 g), chopped
- 1 shallot (about 40 g), finely chopped
- 1/3 cup (85 g) light mayonnaise
- 8 slices whole-grain bread (about 30 g each), toasted
- 8 (15 g) Romaine lettuce leaves
- Salt and freshly ground black pepper

Directions:

1. Combine the salmon, apple, celery, shallot, and mayonnaise in a mixing bowl. Season with salt and pepper.
2. Place 1 slices bread on a plate, top with lettuce and salmon salad, and then covers with another slice of bread. Repeat procedure for the remaining ingredients.
3. Serve and enjoy.

Nutrition:

- **Calories:** 315
- **Fat:** 11.3 g
- **Carbohydrates:** 40.4 g
- **Protein:** 15.1 g

109. SMOKED SALMON AND CHEESE ON RYE BREAD

Easy/Dairy-free/Vegan

Preparation Time: 15 minutes

Cooking time: 10 minutes

Servings: 4

Ingredients:

- 8 ounces (250 g) smoked salmon, thinly sliced
- 1/3 cup (85 g) mayonnaise
- 2 tablespoons (30 ml) lemon juice
- 1 tablespoon (15 g) Dijon mustard
- 1 teaspoon (3 g) garlic, minced
- 4 slices cheddar cheese (about 2 oz. or 30 g each)
- 8 slices rye bread (about 2 oz. or 30 g each)
- 8 (15 g) Romaine lettuce leaves
- Salt and freshly ground black pepper

Directions:

1. Mix together the mayonnaise, lemon juice, mustard, and garlic in a small bowl. Flavor with salt and pepper and set aside.
2. Spread dressing on 4 bread slices. Top with lettuce, salmon, and cheese. Cover with remaining rye bread slices.
3. Serve and enjoy.

Nutrition:

Calories: 365

Fat: 16.6 g

Carbohydrates: 31.6 g

Protein: 18.8 g

Sodium: 951 mg

110.   PAN-FRIED TROUT

Easy/Gluten-free/Vegan

Preparation time: 15 minutes

Cooking time: 10 minutes

Servings: 4

Ingredients:

- 1 ¼ pounds trout fillets
- 1/3 cup white, or yellow, cornmeal
- ¼ teaspoon anise seeds
- ¼ teaspoon black pepper
- ½ cup minced cilantro, or parsley
- Vegetable cooking spray
- Lemon wedges

Directions:

1. Coat fish with combined cornmeal, spices, and cilantro, pressing it gently into fish. Spray a large skillet with cooking spray; heat over medium heat until hot. Add fish and cook until fish is tender and flakes with a fork, about 5 minutes on each side. Serve with lemon wedges.

Nutrition:

- **Calories:** 207
- **Total Carbohydrate:** 19 g
- **Cholesterol:** 27 mg
- **Total Fat:** 16 g
- **Fiber:** 4 g
- **Protein:** 18g

111.   GREEK TUNA SALAD BITES

Easy/Dairy-Free

Preparation Time: 5 Minutes

Cooking Time: 10 Minutes

Servings: 6

Ingredients:

- Cucumbers (2 medium)
- White tuna (2-6 oz. cans.)
- Lemon juice (half of 1 lemon)

- Red bell pepper (.5 cup)
- Sweet/red onion (.25 cup)
- Black olives (.25 cup)
- Garlic (2 tablespoon)
- Olive oil (2 tablespoon)
- Fresh parsley (2 tablespoon)
- Dried oregano - salt & pepper (as desired)

Direction:

1. Drain and flake the tuna. Juice the lemon. Dice/chop the onions, olives, pepper, parsley, and garlic. Slice each of the cucumbers into thick rounds (skin off or on).
2. In a mixing container, combine the rest of the fixings.
3. Place a heaping spoonful of salad onto the rounds and enjoy for your next party or just a snack.

Nutrition:

- **Calories:** 400
- **Fats:** 22 g
- **Carbs:** 26 g
- **Fiber Content:** 8 g
- **Protein:** 30 g

112. SOLE WITH ROSEMARY POTATOES

Medium/Dairy-free/Vegan

Preparation time: 15 minutes

Cooking time: 1 hour

Servings: 4

Ingredients:

- 4 small baking potatoes, cut into wedges
- Vegetable cooking spray
- 2 tablespoons dried rosemary leaves
- ½ teaspoon garlic powder
- ¼ teaspoon pepper
- 4 shallots, minced
- 1 small red onion, chopped
- 1 large clove garlic, minced
- 1 ¼ pound sole fillets

Directions:

1. Place potatoes on baking sheet; spray lightly with cooking spray and sprinkle with rosemary, garlic powder, and pepper. Bake potatoes at 400 degrees until fork-tender, about 45 minutes.

2. About 15 minutes before potatoes are done, spray a large skillet with cooking spray; heat over medium heat until hot. Sauté shallots, onion, and garlic until tender, about 5 minutes.

3. Fold each sole fillet in half and add to skillet. Cook fish over medium heat until fish is tender and flakes with a fork, about 6 minutes, turning once.

4. Place fish on serving platter; spoon shallot mixture over fish. Surround with hot rosemary potatoes.

Nutrition:

- **Calories:** 279
- **Cholesterol:** 0.2 mg
- **Total Fat:** 16 g
- **Fiber:** 2 g
- **Protein:** 30 g

113.   SARDINES ON CRACKERS

Easy/Gluten-free

Preparation time: 5 minutes

Cooking time: 0

Servings: 4

Ingredients:

- 4 whole-grain Scandinavian-style crackers, such as Wasa, Ry Krisp, Ryvita, Kavli
- 8-12 canned sardines, preferably packed in olive oil
- 4 lemon wedges

Directions:

1. Place 2 to 3 sardines on top of each cracker. Complete with a squeeze of lemon.

Nutrition:

- **Calories:** 64
- **Total Carbohydrate:** 8 g
- **Cholesterol:** 20 mg
- **Total Fat:** 2 g
- **Fiber:** 1 g
- **Protein**: 4 g

114.   SARDINES AND PINEAPPLE SANDWICH TOAST

Easy/Dairy-free

Preparation time: 10 minutes

Cooking time: 15 minutes

Servings: 2

Ingredients:

- 4 slices bread
- 1 tablespoon. mayonnaise
- 1 pinch salt and ground black pepper
- 2 teaspoons. Marmalade
- 4 potato chips, crushed
- 2 pieces' pineapple, thinly sliced
- 4 sardines, drained, or to taste

Directions:

1. Preheat your sandwich maker following the manufacturer's directions.
2. Spread 2 slices of bread with mayonnaise. Coat with marmalade. Scatter potato chips over marmalade. Layer the pineapple over chips.
3. Crumble sardines in a bowl with a fork. Scatter over the top of the pineapple slices. Flavor with pepper and salt; cover with leftover 2 slices of bread.
4. Toast in the prepared sandwich maker until crispy and brown, about 5 minutes.

Nutrition:

- **Calories:** 271
- **Total Carbohydrate:** 33.3 g
- **Cholesterol:** 37 mg
- **Total Fat:** 10.8 g
- **Protein:** 10.1 g

115.   SARDINES WITH GINGER

Easy/Gluten-free

Preparation time: 10 minutes

Cooking time: 16 minutes

Servings: 2

Ingredients:

- 1 teaspoon sesame oil

- 4 fresh sardines
- 3 tablespoons sake
- 2 spring onions, finely chopped
- 1 1/2 tablespoons soy sauce
- 1 1/2 tablespoon mirin (Japanese sweet rice wine)
- 2 teaspoons chopped ginger

Direction:

1. Heat oil over high heat in a skillet. Put in sardines and cook until golden, turning occasionally, about 3 minutes on each side. Remove onto a serving plate.

2. In a small bowl, stir chopped ginger, mirin, soy sauce, spring onions, and sake together to make the sauce. Transfer the sauce over sardines to serve.

Nutrition:

- **Calories:** 451 calories;
- **Total Carbohydrate:** 7 g
- **Cholesterol:** 0 mg
- **Total Fat:** 25.9 g
- **Protein:** 33.9 g

116. SARDINES WITH GRILLED BREAD AND TOMATO

Easy/Gluten-free

Preparation time: 10 minutes

Cooking time: 20 minutes

Servings: 4 Servings

Ingredients:

- 2 tablespoons olive oil, plus more
- 4 (3/4"-thick) slices sourdough or country-style bread
- 12 whole fresh sardines (1–1 1/2 lbs. total), scaled, gutted, large pin bones removed
- Kosher salt, freshly ground pepper
- Freshly ground pepper
- 1 large tomato, preferably heirloom, sliced
- Torn basil leaves (for serving)

Directions:

1. **Preparation**: Set the grill to medium-high heat; grease the grate. Brush 2 tablespoons. of oil total on both sides of bread and grill, flipping from time to time, for about 4 minutes until toasted and lightly charred.

2. Place the grilled bread to a plate.

3. Season the outside and inside of sardines with pepper and salt (no need to grease them, as their skin has so much natural oil). Grill, flipping from time to time, for 5 to 7 minutes until cooked through and lightly charred.

4. Serve sardines with tomato and grilled bread sprinkled with oil and topped with basil.

Nutrition:

- **Calories:** 486
- **Total Carbohydrate:** 74 g
- **Cholesterol:** 18 mg
- **Total Fat:** 12 g
- **Fiber:** 4 g
- **Protein:** 21 g

117.   CURRY TUNA SALAD SNACKERS

Easy/Gluten-free/Vegan

Preparation Time: 10 Minutes

Cooking Time: 10 Minutes

Servings: 4

Ingredients:

- ¼ cup plain, low-fat Greek yogurt
- 1 tablespoon mayonnaise
- 1 teaspoon curry powder
- ¼ teaspoon red pepper flakes
- 1 teaspoon freshly squeezed lemon juice
- 1 (5-ounces) can tuna, drained
- ½ cup diced celery
- ¼ cup shredded carrots
- ¼ cup diced red onion
- ¼ cup chopped dried apricots
- ¼ cup chopped pistachios
- 1 large cucumber, sliced

Direction:

1. In a large bowl, mix the yogurt, mayonnaise, curry powder, red pepper flakes, and lemon juice together.

2. Add the tuna, celery, carrots, red onion, dried apricots, and pistachios to the mixture, and stir to combine and evenly distribute all ingredients.

3. On a serving platter, arrange the sliced cucumbers and scoop the tuna mixture onto each one. Serve immediately or store the mixture and sliced cucumber separately for up to 3 days.

Nutrition:

- **Calories:** 170;
- **Total Fat:** 6 g;
- **Cholesterol:** 20 mg;
- **Carbohydrates:** 15 g;
- **Fiber:** 3 g;
- **Protein:** 15 g

118.   EDAMAME-AVOCADO HUMMUS

Easy/Gluten-free/Vegan

Preparation Time: 10 Minutes

Cooking Time: 10 Minutes

Servings: 4

Ingredients:

- 1 avocado
- 1½ cups frozen shelled edamame, thawed
- ¼ cup chopped fresh cilantro
- 1 scallion, cut into short pieces
- 1 teaspoon onion powder
- 2 tablespoons extra-virgin olive oil
- 1 tablespoon tahini
- Pinch salt
- Pinch freshly ground black pepper

Direction:

1. In the bowl of your food processor, combine the avocado, edamame, cilantro, scallion, onion powder, olive oil, tahini, salt, and pepper.

2. Pulse until the mixture starts to combine, then mix at a high speed until the mixture is smooth.

Nutrition:

- **Calories:** 150;
- **Total Fat:** 7g;

- **Cholesterol:** 25 mg;
- **Cholesterol:** 25 mg;
- **Fiber:** 4 g;
- **Protein:** 10 g

119.   SMOKED SALMON DEVILED EGGS

Easy/Dairy-free

Preparation Time: 5 Minutes

Cooking Time: 10 Minutes

Servings: 4

Ingredients:

- 2 ounces' low-fat cream cheese
- 2 tablespoons mayonnaise
- ½ teaspoon dried dill
- ¼ teaspoon mustard powder
- Pinch salt
- Pinch freshly ground black pepper
- 2 ounces smoked salmon
- Smoked paprika, for garnish (optional)
- Fresh dill, for garnish (optional)

Direction:

1. Halve each egg lengthwise. Remove the yolks and add to a mixing bowl with the cream cheese, mayonnaise, dill, mustard powder, salt, and pepper. Use a fork to mash into a smooth mixture, combining until creamy with no chunks remaining.

2. Spoon the mixture into a zip-top bag and snip a bottom tip off the bag with kitchen shears. Pipe the filling back into the well of each egg white.

3. Flake the smoked salmon apart and layer on top. Garnish with smoked paprika or fresh dill, if desired, and serve.

Nutrition:
- **Calories:** 180;
- **Total Fat:** 7 g;
- **Cholesterol:** 25 mg;
- **Carbohydrates:** 10 g;
- **Fiber:** 4 g;
- **Protein:** 15 g

---

120.   NO-BAKE FRUIT & SEED GRANOLA BARS

Easy/Gluten-free

Preparation Time: 5 Minutes

Cooking Time: 10 Minutes

Servings: 6

Ingredients:
- 1½ cups uncooked rolled oats
- ¾ cup crisped rice cereal
- ¼ cup mini chocolate chips
- ¼ cup pepitas
- ¼ cup ground flaxseed
- ⅓ cup dried cranberries
- 2 tablespoons unsweetened coconut flakes
- ½ teaspoon ground cinnamon
- ¼ teaspoon salt
- ½ cup brown rice syrup
- ¼ cup creamy peanut butter
- 1 teaspoon vanilla extract

Direction:
1. Line a 9-inch-square baking pan with parchment paper. Leave about 1 inch overhanging the edges for easy removal.
2. In a large mixing bowl, combine the oats, crisped rice, chocolate chips, pepitas, flaxseed, cranberries, coconut, cinnamon, and salt.

3. In a small saucepan over low heat, heat the brown rice syrup. Add the peanut butter, and stir until smooth. When the mixture is warm and runny, remove from the heat and add the vanilla. Stir to combine.

4. Pour the syrup mixture over the dry ingredients. Combine until all the ingredients are coated and sticky mixture forms.

5. Scoop the mixture into the prepared pan and spread evenly. Use the back of a spatula or clean, moist hands to press into an even layer. The more tightly packed, the better the bars will hold together.

6. Place the pan in the fridge, uncovered, for at least 30 minutes to set. Remove by pulling upward on the parchment paper and transfer it to a cutting board. Slice into 12 even bars.

7. Store in an airtight container in the refrigerator with a single sheet of parchment or wax paper between layers for up to 1 week. Store in the freezer by individually wrapping each bar and placing it in a freezer-safe sealed bag. Thaw overnight in the fridge.

Nutrition:
- **Calories:** 160;
- **Total Fat:** 6 g;
- **Cholesterol:** 25 mg;
- **Carbohydrates:** 10 g;
- **Fiber:** 3 g;
- **Sugars:** 8 g;
- **Protein:** 10 g

121.   LIGHT CHEESE NACHOS

Easy/Dairy-free

Preparation Time: 5 Minutes

Cooking Time: 15 Minutes

Servings: 4

Ingredients:
- Reduced-fat tortilla chips (2 oz./about 28 chips)
- Reduced-fat Mexican cheese blend (.5 cup)
- Red onion (half of 1 small)
- Red bell pepper (half of 1 small)
- Prepared salsa (.25 cup)
- Plain, non-fat Greek yogurt (.25 cup)
- Cilantro (1 tablespoon.)

- Black olives (1 tablespoon.)
- Jalapeno slices (2 tablespoons.)

Direction:

1. Dice the onion, peppers, and cilantro. Slice the olives.
2. Arrange the chips on a microwave-safe plate and garnish with the cheese.
3. Set the timer for one minute using the high setting.
4. Top and serve with the rest of the fixings immediately.

Nutrition:

- **Calories:** 238
- **Fats:** 10 g
- **Fiber Content:** 2 g
- **Protein:** 13 g

122.   **MARINATED OLIVES & CHEESE**

Easy/Dairy-free

Preparation Time: 5 Minutes

Cooking Time: 10 Minutes

Servings: 4

Ingredients:

- Spanish olives (6 oz.)
- Small black olives (6 oz.)
- Fire-roasted peppers (.33 cup)
- Dubliner cheese — ex. Kerrygold (.33 cup)
- Red onion (.33 cup)
- Cloves of garlic (2)
- Capers (1 tablespoon.)
- Lemon juice (1 tablespoon.)
- Oil (3 tablespoons)
- Red wine vinegar (2 tablespoons)
- Italian seasoning (1 teaspoon)
- Red pepper flakes 1 pinch)

Direction:

1. Dice the peppers, onion, and garlic
2. Combine each of the fixings and chill overnight for the best results or at least for two hours.

3. Note: You can also use Swiss or parmesan cheese.

4. Serve with crusty bread and a glass of wine for a super afternoon snack.

Nutrition:

- **Calories:** 220
- **Fats:** 20 g
- **Carbs:** 13 g
- **Fiber Content:** 5 g
- **Protein:** 2 g

123.   CAJUN-STYLE FISH

Easy/Gluten-free

Preparation time: 15 minutes

Cooking time: 25 minutes

Servings: 4

Ingredients:

- 1 cup chopped onion
- 1 clove garlic, minced
- 2 teaspoons margarine
- 1 can (15 ½ ounces) diced tomatoes, un-drained
- 1 large green bell pepper, chopped
- 2 cups cubed zucchini and yellow squash
- ½ teaspoon dried basil leaves
- ½ teaspoon dried thyme leaves
- ¼ teaspoon dried marjoram leaves
- 2-3 drops hot pepper sauce
- Salt and pepper, to taste
- Vegetable cooking spray
- 1pound skinless fish fillets (flounder, sole, halibut, turbot, or other lean white fish)
- 3 cups cooked rice, warm

Directions:

1. Sauté onion and garlic in margarine in a large skillet until almost tender, about 5 minutes. Add tomatoes, green pepper, squash, and herbs. Heat to boiling; reduce heat and cook, covered, about 10 minutes or until vegetables are tender. Season to taste with hot pepper sauce, salt, and pepper.

Nutrition:

- **Calories:** 318
- **Cholesterol:** 22 mg
- **Total Fat:** 16 g
- **Fiber:** 2 g
- **Protein:** 19 g

124.   MINI ZUCCHINI PIZZAS

Easy/Gluten-free

Preparation Time: 5 Minutes

Cooking Time: 10 Minutes

Servings: 4

Ingredients:

- Zucchini (1-2 large)
- Mozzarella cheese (.5 cup)
- Pizza/marinara sauce (.5 cup)
- Black olives (.5 cup)

Direction:

1. Slice the zucchini into circles and pour the sauce over each serving.

2. Top with olives and cheese.

3. Broil a few minutes until it's nicely browned.

Nutrition:

- **Calories:** 50
- **Fats:** 3 g
- **Carbs:** 3 g
- **Protein:** 3 g

Chapter 11. FAST AND CHEAP

125.   CREAMED COCONUT CURRY SPINACH

Easy/Gluten-free

Preparation Time: 30 minutes

Cooking time: 30 seconds

Servings: 6

Ingredients:

- 1-pound frozen spinach, thawed and drained of moisture
- 1 small can whole fat coconut milk
- 2 teaspoons yellow curry paste
- 1 teaspoon lemon zest
- Cashews for garnish

Directions:

1. Heat a medium-sized pan to medium-high heat, then add the curry paste and cook for 30 seconds. Add a small amount of the coconut milk and stir to combine and then cook until the paste is aromatic.

2. Add the spinach, and then season. Separate the rest of the ingredients from the cashews, and allow the sauce to reduce slightly.

3. Keep the sauce creamy, but reduce it to coat the spinach well. Serve with chopped cashews.

Nutrition:

- **Calories:** 191
- **Total Carbohydrate:** 9 g
- **Cholesterol:** 2 mg
- **Total Fat:** 14 g
- **Fiber:** 1 g
- **Protein:** 4 g

126.   SHRIMP SALAD COCKTAILS

Medium/Dairy-free

Preparation time: 35 minutes

Cooking time: 35 minutes

Servings: 8 servings

Ingredients:

- 2 cups mayonnaise

- 1/4 cup ketchup
- 1/4 cup lemon juice
- 1 tablespoon. Worcestershire sauce
- 2 lbs. peeled and deveined cooked large shrimp
- 2 celery ribs, finely chopped
- 3 tablespoons. minced fresh tarragon or 3 teaspoons dried tarragon
- 1/4 teaspoon. salt 1/4 teaspoon pepper
- 2 cups shredded romaine
- 2 cups seedless red and green grapes, halved
- 6 plum tomatoes, seeded and finely chopped
- 1/2 cup chopped peeled mango or papaya
- Minced chives or parsley

Directions:

1. Combine Worcestershire sauce, lemon juice, ketchup, and mayonnaise together in a small bowl. Combine pepper, salt, tarragon, celery, and shrimp together in a large bowl. Put in 1 cup of dressing toss well to coat.

2. Scoop 1 tablespoon. of the dressing into 8 cocktail glasses. Layer each glass with 1/4 cup of lettuce, followed by 1/2 cup of the shrimp mixture, 1/4 cup of grapes, 1/3 cup of tomatoes, and finally 1 tablespoon of mango. Spread the remaining dressing over the top; sprinkle chives on top. Serve immediately.

Nutrition:

- **Calories:** 580
- **Total Carbohydrate:** 16 g
- **Cholesterol:** 192 mg
- **Total Fat:** 46 g
- **Fiber:** 2 g
- **Protein:** 24 g

---

127.   GARLIC CHIVE CAULIFLOWER MASH

Easy/Dairy-free/Vegan

Preparation Time: 20 minutes

Cooking time: 18 minutes

Servings: 5

Ingredients:

- 4 cups cauliflower
- 1/3 cup vegetarian mayonnaise
- 1 garlic clove
- 1/2 teaspoon. kosher salt
- 1 tablespoon. water
- 1/8 teaspoon. pepper
- 1/4 teaspoon. lemon juice
- 1/2 teaspoon lemon zest
- 1 tablespoon Chives, minced

Directions:

1. In a bowl that is safe to microwave, add the cauliflower, mayo, garlic, water, and salt/pepper and mix until the cauliflower is well coated. Cook on high for 15-18 minutes, until the cauliflower is almost mushy.

2. Blend the mixture in a strong blender until completely smooth, adding a little more water if the mixture is too chunky. Season with the remaining ingredients and serve.

Nutrition:

- **Calories:** 178
- **Total Carbohydrate:** 14 g
- **Cholesterol:** 18 mg
- **Total Fat:** 18 g
- **Fiber:** 4 g
- **Protein:** 2 g

128.   BEET GREENS WITH PINE NUTS GOAT CHEESE

Easy/Gluten-free

Preparation Time: 25 minutes

Cooking time: 15 minutes

Servings: 3

Ingredients:

- 4 cups beet tops, washed and chopped roughly
- 1 teaspoon. EVOO
- 1 tablespoon. no sugar added balsamic vinegar
- 2 oz. crumbled dry goat cheese

- 2 tablespoons. Toasted pine nuts

Directions:

1. Warm the oil in a large pan, then cook the beet greens on medium-high heat until they release their moisture. Let it cook until almost tender. Flavor with salt and pepper and remove from heat.

2. Toss the greens in a mixture of balsamic vinegar and olive oil, then top with nuts and cheese. Serve warm.

Nutrition:

- **Calories:** 215
- **Total Carbohydrate:** 4 g
- **Cholesterol:** 12 mg
- **Total Fat:** 18 g
- **Fiber: 2 g**
- **Protein:** 10 g

129.   SHRIMP WITH DIPPING SAUCE

Easy/Gluten-free

Preparation time: 5 minutes

Cooking time: 15 minutes

Serving: 6

Ingredients:

- 1 tablespoon. reduced-sodium soy sauce
- 2 teaspoons. Hot pepper sauce
- 1 teaspoon. canola oil
- 1/4 teaspoon. garlic powder
- 1/8 to 1/4 teaspoon. cayenne pepper
- 1 lb. uncooked medium shrimp, peeled and deveined
- 2 tablespoons. Chopped green onions

DIPPING SAUCE:

- 3 tablespoons Reduced-sodium soy sauce
- 1 teaspoon. rice vinegar
- 1 tablespoon. orange juice
- 2 teaspoons. Sesame oil
- 2 teaspoons. Honey
- 1 garlic clove, minced

- 1-1/2 teaspoons. Minced fresh ginger root

Directions:

1. Heat the initial 5 ingredients in a big nonstick frying pan for 30 seconds, then mix continuously.
2. Add onions and shrimp and stir fry for 4-5 minutes or until the shrimp turns pink. Mix together the sauce ingredients and serve it with the shrimp.

Nutrition:

- **Calories:** 97
- **Total Carbohydrate:** 4 g
- **Cholesterol:** 112 mg
- **Total Fat:** 3 g
- **Protein:** 13 g
- **Fiber:** 0 g

130.   CELERIAC CAULIFLOWER MASH

Easy/Dairy-free

Preparation Time: 20 minutes

Cooking time: 12 minutes

Servings: 6

Ingredients:

- 1 head cauliflower
- 1 small celery root
- 1/4 cup butter
- 1 tablespoon. chopped rosemary

- 1 tablespoon. chopped thyme
- 1 cup cream cheese

Directions:

1. Skin the celery root and cut it into small pieces. Cut the cauliflower into similar sized pieces and combine.
2. Toast the herbs in the butter in a large pan until they become fragrant. Add the cauliflower and celery root and stir to combine. Season and cook at medium-high until whatever moisture is in the vegetable releases itself, then cover and cook on low for 10-12 minutes.
3. Once the vegetables are soft, remove from the heat and place them in the blender. Make it smooth, then put the cream cheese and puree again. Season and serve.

Nutrition:

- **Calories:** 225
- **Total Carbohydrate:** 4 g
- **Cholesterol:** 1 mg
- **Total Fat:** 20 g
- **Fiber:** 0 g
- **Protein:** 5 g

---

131. <u>**CHEDDAR DROP BISCUITS**</u>

Easy/Dairy-free

Preparation Time: 30 minutes

Cooking time: 15 minutes

Servings: 8

Ingredients:

- 1/4 cup coconut oil
- 4 eggs
- 2 teaspoon apple cider vinegar
- 1 1/2 cup coarse almond meal
- 1/2 teaspoon. baking powder, gluten-free
- 1/2 teaspoon. onion powder
- 1/4 teaspoon. salt
- 3/4 cup cheddar cheese
- 2 tablespoons. Chopped jalapenos

Directions:

1. Line a sheet tray with parchment paper, and then preheat the oven to 400F
2. Mix the wet ingredients in a bowl until combined, then reserve. Mix the dry ingredients in a separate bowl until combined, and then add them to the wet ingredients, stirring until incorporated. Fold in the cheddar cheese and jalapenos.
3. Drop the dough onto the parchment paper into eight roughly equal pieces, and then shape as desired once they are on the tray.
4. Bake until golden brown, 12-15 minutes. Rotate the tray halfway through baking so browning is even.
5. Cool slightly and serve.

Nutrition:

- **Calories:** 260
- **Total Carbohydrate:** 4 g
- **Cholesterol:** 8 mg
- **Total Fat:** 22 g
- **Fiber:** 1 g
- **Protein:** 4 g

132.   ROASTED RADISH WITH FRESH HERBS

Easy/Gluten-free

Preparation Time: 15 minutes

Cooking time: 10 minutes

Servings: 4

Ingredients:

- 1 tablespoon. coconut oil
- 1 bunch radishes
- 2 tablespoons. Minced chives
- 1 tablespoon. minced rosemary
- 1 tablespoon. minced thyme

Directions:

1. Wash the radishes, and then remove the tops and stems. Cut them into quarters and reserve.
2. Add the oil to a cast iron pan, then heat to medium. Add the radishes, and then season with salt and pepper. Cook on medium heat for 6-8 minutes, until almost tender, then add the herbs and cook through.
3. The radishes can be served warm with meats or chilled with salads.

Nutrition:

- **Calories:** 123
- **Total Carbohydrate:** 6 g
- **Cholesterol:** 8 mg
- **Total Fat:** 13 g
- **Fiber:** 2 g
- **Protein:** 6 g

133.   SUMMER BRUSCHETTA

Medium/Gluten-free

Preparation Time: 15 min

Cooking Time: 3 hours

Servings: 4

Ingredients:

- Basil leaves (chopped) – 6
- Artichoke hearts (quartered) – ½ cup
- Kalamata olives (halved) – ¼ cup
- Capers – ¼ cup
- Roma tomatoes (diced) – 4
- Balsamic vinegar – 3 tablespoons
- Avocado oil – 3 tablespoons
- Onion powder – ¾ teaspoon
- Sea salt – ¾ teaspoon
- Black pepper – ½ teaspoon
- Garlic (minced) – 2 tablespoons

Directions:

1. Combine all the ingredients in the slow cooker and stir the mix.
2. Cook for 3 hours on high, stirring the mix after every hour.

Nutrition:

- **Calories:** 152
- **Total Carbohydrate:** 4 g
- **Cholesterol:** 1 mg
- **Total Fat:** 13 g
- **Fiber:** 4 g

- **Protein:** 1 g
- **Sodium:** 140 mg

134. TOMATO CHEDDAR FONDUE

Medium/Dairy-free

Preparation time: 20 minutes

Cooking time: 30 minutes

Serving: 3-1/2 cups

Ingredients:

- 1 garlic clove, halved
- 6 medium tomatoes, seeded and diced
- 2/3 cup dry white wine
- 6 tablespoons. butter, cubed
- 1-1/2 teaspoons. dried basil
- Dash cayenne pepper
- 2 cups shredded cheddar cheese
- 1 tablespoon. all-purpose flour
- Cubed French bread and cooked shrimp

Directions:

1. Rub the bottom and sides of a fondue pot with a garlic clove. Set aside and discard the garlic.
2. Combine wine, butter, basil, cayenne, and tomatoes in a large saucepan. On medium-low heat, bring mixture to a simmer, then decrease the heat to low. Mix cheese with flour. Add to tomato mixture gradually while stirring after each addition until cheese is melted.
3. Pour into the preparation fondue pot and keep warm. Enjoy with shrimp and bread cubes.

Nutrition:

- **Calories:** 118
- **Total Carbohydrate:** 4 g
- **Cholesterol:** 30 mg
- **Total Fat:** 10 g
- **Fiber:** 1 g
- **Protein**: 4 g

135. SWISS SEAFOOD CANAPÉS

Medium/Gluten-free

Preparation time: 20 minutes

Cooking time: 25 minutes

Servings: 4 dozen.

Ingredients:

- 1 can (6 oz.) small shrimp, rinsed and drained
- 1 package (6 oz.) frozen crabmeat, thawed
- 1 cup shredded Swiss cheese
- 2 hard-boiled large eggs, chopped
- 1/4 cup finely chopped celery
- 1/4 cup mayonnaise
- 1/4 cup French salad dressing or seafood cocktail sauce
- 2 green onions, chopped
- Dash salt
- 1 loaf (16 oz.) snack rye bread

Directions:

1. Mix the first nine ingredients in a large bowl. Put bread on ungreased baking sheets. Broil for 1 to 2 minutes, 4 to 6-inches from the heat, or until lightly browned. Flip slices over; spread 1 rounded tablespoonful of seafood mixture on each. Broil for 4 to 5 more minutes or until heated through.

Nutrition:

- **Calories:** 57
- **Total Carbohydrate:** 5 g
- **Cholesterol:** 22 mg
- **Total Fat:** 3 g
- **Fiber:** 1 g
- **Protein:** 3 g

136.   **SQUASH & ZUCCHINI**

Medium/Gluten-free

Preparation Time: 5 min

Cooking Time: 4-6 hours

Servings: 6

Ingredients:

- Zucchini (sliced and quartered) – 2 cups
- Yellow squash (sliced and quartered) – 2 cups
- Pepper – ¼ teaspoon

- Italian seasoning – 1 teaspoon
- Garlic powder – 1 teaspoon
- Sea salt – ½ teaspoon
- Butter (cubed) – ¼ cup
- Parmesan cheese (grated) – ¼ cup

Directions:

1. Combine all the ingredients in the slow cooker.
2. Cook covered for 4-6 hours on low.

Nutrition:

- **Calories:** 122
- **Total Carbohydrate:** 4 g
- **Cholesterol:** 18 mg
- **Total Fat:** 9.9 g
- **Fiber:** 4 g
- **Protein:** 14 g

137.   TASTY SHRIMP SPREAD

Easy/Gluten-free

Preparation time: 15 minutes

Cooking time: 20 minutes

Serving: 2-1/2 cups

Ingredients:

- 1 package (8 oz.) cream cheese, softened
- 1/4 cup butter, softened
- 1/4 cup mayonnaise
- 1/2 lb. peeled and deveined cooked shrimp, finely chopped
- 1 medium onion, chopped
- Assorted crackers and fresh vegetables

Directions:

1. Combine mayonnaise, butter, and cream cheese together in a small bowl. Mix in onion and shrimp. Refrigerate with a cover till serving.
2. Serve with crackers and vegetables if you want.

Nutrition:

- **Calories:** 189

- **Cholesterol:** 73 mg
- **Total Fat:** 17 g
- **Fiber:** 0 g
- **Protein:** 7 g

138.   CREAMY COCONUT SPINACH

Easy/Dairy-free

Preparation Time: 10 min

Cooking Time: 25 min

Servings: 2

Ingredients:

- Baby spinach – 4 cups
- Coconut milk – ¼ cup
- Nutmeg – 1/8 teaspoon
- Granulated sugar substitute – 2 teaspoons
- Cayenne pepper — 1/8 teaspoon
- Salt – to taste

Directions:

1. Heat a saucepan and warm the coconut milk in it for 2 minutes.
2. Mix in the spinach, cooking until bright green and wilted.
3. Mix in the rest of the ingredients.

Nutrition:

- **Calories:** 73
- **Total Carbohydrate:** 4 g
- **Cholesterol:** 0 mg
- **Total Fat:** 7 g
- **Fiber:** 4 g
- **Protein:** 4 g

Chapter 12. RECIPES FOR KIDS

139.   <u>RICE SOUP WITH FISH & GINGER</u>

Medium/Gluten-free

Preparation Time: 10 minutes

Cooking Time: 30 minutes

Servings: 4

Ingredients:

- 1 red onion
- 2/4 lbs. white fish

MARINADE

- ½ tsp salt
- 1 scallion
- ½ tsp sugar
- 1 tablespoon canola oil
- 1 tablespoon fish sauce
- 2 tablespoons cider vinegar
- 2 tablespoons ginger
- 2 tablespoons cilantro
- 6 cups of rice

Directions:

1. In a bowl mix the following marinade Ingredients: ginger, cilantro, salt, sugar, fish sauce, oil and add fish and onion, set aside

2. In a saucepan, bring to boil the rice soup, divide the fish among the soup bowl

3. Garnish with scallion and serve.

Nutrition:

- **Calories:** 189
- **Cholesterol:** 43 mg
- **Total Fat:** 17 g
- **Fiber:** 0 g
- **Protein:** 7 g

140. PRAWN NOODLE SALAD

Easy/Gluten-free/Vegan

Preparation Time: 10 minutes

Cooking Time: 10 minutes

Servings: 4

Ingredients:

- ¼ lb. noodle
- ¼ lb. baby spinach
- 3 oz. cooked prawn
- ¼ lb. snap pea
- 1 carrot

DRESSING:

- 1 red chili
- 1 tsp fish sauce
- 1 tablespoon mint
- 2 tablespoons rice vinegar
- 1 tsp sugar

Directions:

1. In a bowl add all dressing ingredients and mix well
2. In another bowl add salad ingredients and mix well, pour dressing over salad and serve.

Nutrition:

- **Calories:** 119
- **Cholesterol:** 33 mg
- **Total Fat:** 17 g
- **Fiber:** 0 g
- **Protein:** 27 g

141. SHRIMP WITH GARLIC

Easy/Gluten-free

Preparation Time: 10 minutes

Cooking Time: 15 minutes

Servings: 4

Ingredients:

- 1 lb. shrimp

- ¼ tsp baking soda
- 2 tablespoons oil
- 2 tsp minced garlic
- ¼ cup vermouth
- 2 tablespoons unsalted butter
- 1 tsp parsley

Directions:

1. In a bowl toss shrimp with baking soda and salt, let it stand for a couple of minutes
2. In a skillet heat olive oil and add shrimp
3. Add garlic, red pepper flakes and cook for 12 minutes
4. Add vermouth and cook for another 45 minutes
5. When ready, remove from heat and serve

Nutrition:

- **Calories:** 129
- **Cholesterol:** 43 mg
- **Total Fat:** 17 g
- **Fiber:** 0 g
- **Protein:** 23 g

142.   SABICH SANDWICH

Easy/Dairy-free/Vegan

Preparation Time: 5 minutes

Cooking Time: 15 minutes

Servings: 4

Ingredients:

- 2 tomatoes
- Olive oil
- ½ lb. eggplant
- ¼ cucumber
- 1 tablespoon lemon juice
- 1 tablespoon parsley
- ¼ head cabbage
- 2 tablespoons wine vinegar
- 2 pita bread
- ½ cup hummus
- ¼ tahini sauce
- 2 hardboiled eggs

Directions:

1. In a skillet fry eggplant slices until tender
2. In a bowl add tomatoes, cucumber, parsley, lemon juice, and season salad
3. In another bowl toss cabbage with vinegar
4. In each pita pocket add hummus, eggplant and drizzle tahini sauce
5. Top with eggs, tahini sauce, and salad

Nutrition:

- **Calories:** 289
- **Cholesterol:** 73 mg
- **Total Fat:** 17 g
- **Fiber:** 0 g
- **Protein:** 17 g

143.   SALMON WITH VEGETABLES

Easy/Gluten-free/Vegan

Preparation Time: 10 minutes

Cooking Time: 15 minutes

Servings: 5

Ingredients:

- 2 tablespoons olive oil
- 2 carrots
- 1 head fennel
- 2 squash
- ¼ onion
- 1inch ginger
- 1 cup white wine
- 2 cups of water
- 2 parsley sprigs
- 2 tarragon sprigs
- 6 oz. salmon fillets
- 1 cup cherry tomatoes
- 1 scallion

Directions:

1. In a skillet heat olive oil, add fennel, squash, onion, ginger, carrot and cook until vegetables are soft
2. Add wine, water, parsley and cook for another 45 minutes
3. Season salmon fillets and place in the pan
4. Cook for 45 minutes per side or until is ready
5. Transfer salmon to a bowl, spoon tomatoes and scallion around salmon and serve

Nutrition:

- **Calories:** 229
- **Cholesterol:** 73 mg
- **Total Fat:** 17 g
- **Fiber:** 0 g
- **Protein:** 37 g

144.   CRISPY FISH

Easy/Gluten-free

Preparation Time: 5 minutes

Cooking Time: 15 minutes

Servings: 4

Ingredients:

- 4 thick fish fillets
- ¼ cup all-purpose flour
- 1 egg
- 1 cup bread crumbs
- 2 tablespoons vegetables
- Lemon wedges

Directions:

1. In a dish add flour, egg, breadcrumbs in different dishes and set aside
2. Dip each fish fillet into the flour, egg, and then bread crumbs bowl
3. Place each fish fillet in a heated skillet and cook for 45 minutes per side
4. When ready remove from pan and serve with lemon wedges

Nutrition:

- **Calories:** 221
- **Cholesterol:** 43 mg
- **Total Fat:** 17 g
- **Fiber:** 0 g
- **Protein:** 22 g

145.   CREAMED COCONUT CURRY SPINACH

Easy/Dairy-free/Vegan

Preparation Time: 30 minutes

Cooking time: 30 seconds

Servings: 6

Ingredients:

- 1-pound frozen spinach, thawed and drained of moisture
- 1 small can whole fat coconut milk
- 2 teaspoons yellow curry paste
- 1 teaspoon lemon zest
- Cashews for garnish

Directions:

1. Heat a medium-sized pan to medium-high heat, then add the curry paste and cook for 30 seconds. Add a small amount of the coconut milk and stir to combine and then cook until the paste is aromatic.

2. Add the spinach, and then season. Separate the rest of the ingredients from the cashews, and allow the sauce to reduce slightly.

3. Keep the sauce creamy, but reduce it to coat the spinach well. Serve with chopped cashews.

Nutrition:

- **Calories:** 191 kcal.
- **Net carbs**: 3 g
- **Protein:** 4 g
- **Fat:** 18 g

---

146.   **SHRIMP SALAD COCKTAILS**

Medium/Dairy-free

Preparation time: 35 minutes

Cooking time: 35 minutes

Servings: 8 servings

Ingredients:

- 2 cups mayonnaise
- 1/4 cup ketchup
- 1/4 cup lemon juice
- 1 tablespoon Worcestershire sauce
- 2 lbs. peeled and deveined cooked large shrimp
- 2 celery ribs, finely chopped
- 3 tablespoons minced fresh tarragon or 3 teaspoons dried tarragon
- 1/4 teaspoon salt
- 1/4 teaspoon pepper
- 2 cups shredded romaine
- 2 cups seedless red and green grapes, halved
- 6 plum tomatoes, seeded and finely chopped
- 1/2 cup chopped peeled mango or papaya
- Minced chives or parsley

Directions:

1. Combine Worcestershire sauce, lemon juice, ketchup, and mayonnaise in a small bowl. Combine pepper, salt, tarragon, celery, and shrimp in a large bowl. Put in 1 cup of dressing toss well to coat.

2. Scoop 1 tablespoon of the dressing into 8 cocktail glasses. Layer each glass with 1/4 cup of lettuce, followed by 1/2 cup of the shrimp mixture, 1/4 cup of grapes, 1/3 cup of tomatoes, and finally 1 tablespoon of mango. Spread the remaining dressing over top; sprinkle chives on top. Serve immediately.

Nutrition:
- **Calories:** 580
- **Cholesterol:** 192 mg
- **Total Fat:** 46 g
- **Fiber:** 2 g
- **Protein:** 24 g
- **Sodium:** 670 mg

147.   GARLIC CHIVE CAULIFLOWER MASH

Easy/Gluten-free/Vegan

Preparation Time: 20 minutes

Cooking time: 18 minutes

Servings: 5

Ingredients:
- 4 cups cauliflower
- 1/3 cup vegetarian mayonnaise
- 1 garlic clove
- 1/2 teaspoon kosher salt
- 1 tablespoon water
- 1/8 teaspoon pepper
- 1/4 teaspoon lemon juice
- 1/2 teaspoon lemon zest
- 1 tablespoon Chives, minced

Directions:
1. In a bowl that is safe to microwave, add the cauliflower, mayo, garlic, water, and salt/pepper and mix until the cauliflower is well coated. Cook on high for 15-18 minutes, until the cauliflower is almost mushy.
2. Blend the mixture in a strong blender until completely smooth, adding a little more water if the mixture is too chunky. Season with the remaining ingredients and serve.

Nutrition:
- **Calories:** 178 kcal.

- **Net carbs:** 3 g,
- **Protein:** 2 g,
- **Fat:** 18g,

148. BEET GREENS WITH PINE NUTS GOAT CHEESE

Easy/Gluten-free/Vegan

Preparation Time: 25 minutes

Cooking time: 15 minutes

Servings: 3

Ingredients:

- 4 cups beet tops, washed and chopped roughly
- 1 teaspoon EVOO
- 1 tablespoon no sugar added balsamic vinegar
- 2 oz. crumbled dry goat cheese
- 2 tablespoon toasted pine nuts

Directions:

1. Warm the oil in a large pan, then cook the beet greens on medium-high heat until they release their moisture. Let it cook until almost tender. Flavor with salt and pepper and remove from heat.
2. Toss the greens in a mixture of balsamic vinegar and olive oil, then top with nuts and cheese. Serve warm.

Nutrition:

- **Calories:** 215 kcal.
- **Net carbs:** 3.5 g,
- **Protein:** 10 g,
- **Fat:** 18 g,

149. SHRIMP WITH DIPPING SAUCE

Easy/Gluten-free

Preparation time: 5 minutes

Cooking time: 15 minutes

Serving: 6

Ingredients:

- 1 tablespoon reduced-sodium soy sauce
- 2 teaspoons Hot pepper sauce
- 1 teaspoon canola oil

- 1/4 teaspoon garlic powder
- 1/8 to 1/4 teaspoon cayenne pepper
- 1 lb. uncooked medium shrimp, peeled and deveined
- 2 tablespoons Chopped green onions

DIPPING SAUCE:

- 3 tablespoons Reduced-sodium soy sauce
- 1 tablespoon rice vinegar
- 1 tablespoon orange juice
- 2 teaspoons Sesame oil
- 2 teaspoons Honey
- 1 garlic clove, minced
- 1-1/2 teaspoon minced fresh ginger root

Directions:

1. Heat the initial 5 ingredients in a big nonstick frying pan for 30 seconds, then mix continuously. Add onions and shrimp and stir fry for 4-5 minutes or until the shrimp turns pink. Mix together the sauce ingredients and serve it with the shrimp.

Nutrition:

- **Calories:** 97
- **Cholesterol:** 112 mg
- **Total Fat:** 3 g
- **Fiber:** 0 g
- **Protein:** 13 g
- **Sodium:** 588 mg

150. MOULES MARINERS

Medium/Gluten-free

Preparation Time: 10 minutes

Cooking Time: 30 minutes

Servings: 4

Ingredients:

- 2 tablespoons unsalted butter
- 1 leek
- 1 shallot
- 2 cloves garlic

- 2 bay leaves
- 1 cup white wine
- 2 lbs. mussels
- 2 tablespoons mayonnaise
- 1 tablespoon lemon zest
- 2 tablespoons parsley
- 1 sourdough bread

Directions:

1. In a saucepan melt butter, add leeks, garlic, bay leaves, shallot and cook until vegetables are soft
2. Bring to a boil, add mussels, and cook for 12 minutes
3. Transfer mussels to a bowl and cover
4. Whisk in remaining butter with mayonnaise and return mussels to the pot
5. Add lemon juice, parsley lemon zest and stir to combine

Nutrition:

- **Calories:** 189
- **Cholesterol:** 73 mg
- **Total Fat:** 17 g
- **Fiber:** 0 g
- **Protein:** 7 g

151.   STEAMED MUSSELS WITH COCONUT CURRY

Easy/Gluten-free/Vegan

Preparation Time: 10 minutes

Cooking Time: 20 minutes

Servings: 4

Ingredients:

- 6 sprigs cilantro
- 2 cloves garlic
- 2 shallots
- ¼ tsp coriander seeds
- ¼ tsp red chili flakes
- 1 tsp zest
- 1 can coconut milk
- 1 tablespoon vegetable oil

- 1 tablespoon curry paste
- 1 tablespoon brown sugar
- 1 tablespoon fish sauce
- 2 lbs. mussels

Directions:

1. In a bowl combine lime zest, cilantro stems, shallot, garlic, coriander seed, chili, and salt
2. In a saucepan heat oil add, garlic, shallots, pounded paste, and curry paste
3. Cook for 34 minutes, add coconut milk, sugar, and fish sauce
4. Bring to a simmer and add mussels
5. Stir in lime juice, cilantro leaves and cook for a couple of more minutes
6. When ready remove from heat and serve

Nutrition:

- **Calories:** 212
- **Cholesterol:** 73 mg
- **Total Fat:** 17 g
- **Fiber:** 0 g
- **Protein:** 27 g

152.   **TUNA NOODLE CASSEROLE**

Easy/Gluten-free/Vegan

Preparation Time: 10 minutes

Cooking Time: 20 minutes

Servings: 4

Ingredients:

- 2 oz. egg noodles
- 4 oz. fraiche
- 1 egg
- 1 tsp cornstarch
- 1 tablespoon juice from 1 lemon
- 1 can tuna
- 1 cup peas
- ¼ cup parsley

Directions:

1. Place noodles in a saucepan with water and bring to a boil

2. In a bowl combine egg, Crème Fraiche, and lemon juice, whisk well

3. When noodles are cooked, add Crème Fraiche mixture to skillet and mix well

4. Add tuna, peas, parsley lemon juice and mix well

5. When ready remove from heat and serve

Nutrition:

- **Calories:** 202
- **Cholesterol:** 33 mg
- **Total Fat:** 17 g
- **Fiber:** 0 g
- **Protein:** 27 g

153.   SALMON BURGERS

Easy/Gluten-free

Preparation Time: 10 minutes

Cooking Time: 20 minutes

Servings: 4

Ingredients:

- 1 lb. salmon fillets
- 1 onion
- ¼ dill fronds
- 1 tablespoon honey
- 1 tablespoon horseradish
- 1 tablespoon mustard

- 1 tablespoon olive oil
- 2 toasted split rolls
- 1 avocado

Directions:

1. Place salmon fillets in a blender and blend until smooth, transfer to a bowl, add onion, dill, honey, horseradish and mix well
2. Season with salt and pepper and form 4 patties
3. In a bowl combine mustard, honey, mayonnaise, and dill
4. In a skillet, heat oil add salmon patties and cook for 23 minutes per side
5. When ready, remove from heat
6. Divided lettuce and onion between the buns
7. Place salmon patty on top and spoon mustard mixture and avocado slices
8. Serve when ready

Nutrition:

- **Calories:** 189
- **Cholesterol:** 73 mg
- **Total Fat:** 17 g
- **Fiber:** 0 g
- **Protein:** 7 g

154.   NIÇOISE SALAD

Easy/Gluten-free/Vegan

Preparation Time: 10 minutes

Cooking Time: 30 minutes

Servings: 4

Ingredients:

- 1 oz. red potatoes
- 1 package green beans
- 2 eggs
- ½ cup tomatoes
- 2 tablespoons wine vinegar
- ¼ tsp salt
- ½ tsp pepper
- ½ tsp thyme

- ¼ cup olive oil
- 6 oz. tuna
- ¼ cup Kalamata olives

Directions:

1. In a bowl combine all ingredients together
2. Add salad dressing and serve

Nutrition:

- **Calories:** 234
- **Cholesterol:** 36 mg
- **Total Fat:** 15 g
- **Fiber:** 0 g
- **Protein:** 22 g

155. SHRIMP CURRY

Medium/Gluten-free

Preparation Time: 10 minutes

Cooking Time: 30 minutes

Servings: 4

Ingredients:

- 2 tablespoons peanut oil
- ¼ onion
- 2 cloves garlic
- 1 tsp ginger
- 1 tsp cumin
- 1 tsp turmeric
- 1 tsp paprika
- ¼ red chili powder
- 1 can tomatoes
- 1 can coconut milk
- 1 lb. peeled shrimp
- 1 tablespoon cilantro

Directions:

1. In a skillet add onion and cook for 45 minutes
2. Add ginger, cumin, garlic, chili, paprika and cook on low heat

3. Pour the tomatoes, coconut milk and simmer for 1012 minutes

4. Stir in shrimp, cilantro, and cook for 23 minutes

5. When ready remove and serve

Nutrition:

- **Calories:** 239
- **Cholesterol:** 73 mg
- **Total Fat:** 17 g
- **Fiber:** 0 g
- **Protein:** 23 g

156.   SALMON PASTA

Easy/Gluten-free

Preparation Time: 10 minutes

Cooking Time: 25 minutes

Servings: 10

Ingredients:

- 5 tablespoons butter
- ¼ onion
- 1 tablespoon all-purpose flour
- 1 tsp garlic powder
- 2 cups skim milk
- ¼ cup Romano cheese
- 1 cup green peas
- ¼ cup canned mushrooms
- 8 oz. salmon
- 1 package penne pasta

Directions:

1. Bring a pot with water to a boil

2. Add pasta and cook for 1012 minutes

3. In a skillet melt butter, add onion and sauté until tender

4. Stir in garlic powder, flour, milk, and cheese

5. Add mushrooms, peas and cook on low heat for 45 minutes

6. Toss in salmon and cook for another 23 minutes

7. When ready serve with cooked pasta

Nutrition:

- **Calories:** 267
- **Cholesterol:** 53 mg
- **Total Fat:** 27 g
- **Fiber:** 0 g
- **Protein:** 35 g

Chapter 13. MAIN FOR EVENTS

157.   LIME GARLIC ROASTED ASPARAGUS

Easy/Gluten-free/Vegan

Preparation time: 5 minutes

Cooking time: 10 minutes

Servings: 2

Ingredients:

- 8 ounces' asparagus
- ½ teaspoon minced garlic
- ¼ of lime, zested, sliced
- 1 tablespoon olive oil
- 2 tablespoons grated parmesan cheese

EXTRA:

- 1/3 teaspoon salt
- ¼ teaspoon ground black pepper
- 1/8 teaspoon dried thyme
- ¼ teaspoon onion powder

Directions:

1. Switch on the oven, then set it to 425 degrees F and let it preheat.
2. Meanwhile, take a medium baking sheet, line it with a parchment sheet, and then spread evenly on it.
3. Drizzle asparagus with ½ tablespoon oil and then sprinkle with lime zest, salt, black pepper, thyme, and onion powder.
4. Top asparagus with lime slices and then bake for 5 minutes, tossing halfway.
5. Then stir together garlic and remaining oil, drizzle this mixture over asparagus, toss until mixed, and then continue baking for 2 minutes.
6. When done, sprinkle cheese on top of asparagus and then serve.

Directions extra:

1. Cool the roasted asparagus and then divide evenly between two meal prep containers. Sprinkle cheese over asparagus, cover with a lid and then store the containers in the refrigerator for up to 5 days. When ready to eat, reheat in the microwave oven for 1 to 2 minutes until hot and then serve.

Nutrition:

- **Calories:** 115;
- **Fats:** 8 g;

- **Protein:** 3 g;
- **Carb:** 5 g;
- **Fiber:** 2 g

---

158.   EGGPLANT STACKS

Easy/Gluten-free/Vegan

Preparation time: 5 minutes

Cooking time: 10 minutes

Servings: 2

Ingredients:

- ½ pound eggplant
- ½ teaspoon dried thyme
- ½ teaspoon dried oregano
- 2 tablespoons olive oil
- 4 tablespoons grated parmesan cheese

EXTRA:

- ½ teaspoon salt
- ½ teaspoon ground black pepper

Directions:

1. Cut eggplant into 1inch thick slices, brush them with oil and then sprinkle with salt, black pepper, thyme, and oregano on both until well-seasoned.
2. Take a grill pan, place it over medium heat, grease it with oil and when hot, place seasoned eggplant slices on it, and then grill for 3 to 4 minutes per side until tender.
3. Then top eggplant slices with cheese, cover with a lid, and grill for 1 to 2 minutes until cheese has melted.
4. Serve straight away.

Directions extra:

1. Cool the eggplant slices, divide them evenly between two meal prep containers, and then store the containers in the refrigerator for up to 5 days. When ready to eat, reheat in the microwave oven for 1 to 2 minutes until hot and then serve.

Nutrition:

- **Calories:** 200;
- **Fats:** 17 g;
- **Protein:** 4 g;

- **Carb:** 7 g;
- **Fiber:** 3 g

159.   TERIYAKI EGGPLANT

Easy/Gluten-free/Vegan

Preparation time: 5 minutes

Cooking time: 15 minutes

Servings: 2

Ingredients:

- ½ pound eggplant
- 1 green onion, chopped
- ½ teaspoon grated ginger
- ½ teaspoon minced garlic
- 1/3 cup soy sauce

EXTRA:

- 1 tablespoon coconut sugar
- ½ tablespoon apple cider vinegar
- 1 tablespoon olive oil

Directions:

1. Prepare teriyaki sauce and for this, take a medium bowl, add ginger, garlic, soy sauce, vinegar, and sugar in it and then whisk until sugar has dissolved completely.
2. Cut eggplant into cubes, add them into teriyaki sauce, toss until well coated, and marinate for 10 minutes.
3. When ready to cook, take a grill pan, place it over medium-high heat, grease it with oil, and when hot, add marinated eggplant.
4. Cook for 3 to 4 minutes per side until nicely browned and beginning to charred, drizzling with excess marinade frequently and transfer to a plate.
5. Sprinkle green onion on top of the eggplant and then serve.

Directions extra:

1. Cool the eggplant, divide evenly between two meal prep containers, and cover with a lid and then store the containers in the refrigerator for up to 7 days. When ready to eat, reheat soup in the microwave oven for 1 to 2 minutes until hot and then serve.

Nutrition:

- **Calories:** 132
- **Fats:** 4 g

- **Protein:** 13.2 g
- **Carb:** 4 g

160. SCALLOPED POTATOES

Medium/Gluten-free

Preparation time: 10 minutes

Cooking time: 30 minutes

Servings: 1

Ingredients:

- 1 1/3 tablespoon flour
- 3 potatoes, peeled, sliced
- 2 green onions, sliced
- 6 tablespoons almond milk, unsweetened
- 3 tablespoons grated parmesan cheese

EXTRA:

- ¼ teaspoon salt
- ¼ teaspoon ground black pepper

Directions:

1. Switch on the oven, then set it to 350 degrees F and let it preheat.
2. Meanwhile, take a small saucepan, place it over medium-low heat, add butter and when it melts, stir in flour until smooth sauce comes together and then stir in salt and black pepper. Whisk in milk until smooth, then remove the pan from heat and stir in 2 tablespoons cheese until melted.
3. Take a baking pan, grease it with oil, line its bottom with some of the potato slices, and sprinkle with one-third of green onion, and cover with one-third of the sauce.
4. Create two more layers by using remaining potatoes, green onion, and sauce, and sprinkle cheese on top.
5. Cover baking pan with foil, bake for 20 minutes, uncover the pan and continue cooking for 5 minutes until the top has turned golden brown. Serve straight away.
6. Cool the scalloped potatoes in the baking pan completely, and then cover with cling film and in the refrigerator for up to 7 days. When ready to eat, transfer scallop potatoes to a heatproof plate, reheat in the microwave oven for 1 to 2 minutes until hot, and then serve.

Nutrition:

- **Calories:** 308;
- **Fats:** 5 g;
- **Protein:** 42 g;

- **Carb:** 7 g;
- **Fiber:** 2 g

161. <u>GREEN ONION STIR-FRY</u>

Easy/Gluten-free/Vegan

Preparation time: 5 minutes

Cooking time: 10 minutes

Servings: 2

Ingredients:

- 2 green onions, sliced, whites and greens separated
- 4 ounces sliced mushrooms
- ½ teaspoon minced garlic
- 1 teaspoon soy sauce
- 1 tablespoon olive oil

EXTRA:

- 1/3 teaspoon salt
- ¼ teaspoon ground black pepper
- ¼ teaspoon red pepper flakes

Directions:

1. Take a medium skillet pan, place it over medium heat, add oil and when hot, add half of the whites of onion and then cook for 2 minutes until softened.
2. Add remaining green onions along with garlic and mushrooms, stir well and then cook for 2 to 3 minutes until mushrooms have turned golden brown and tender.

3. Drizzle with soy sauce, sprinkle with salt, black pepper, and red pepper flakes, stir until mixed and continue cooking for 1 minute until thoroughly heated.

4. Serve straight away.

5. Cool, the mushrooms divide evenly between two meal prep containers, cover with a lid, and then store the containers in the refrigerator for up to 7 days. When ready to eat, reheat mushrooms in the microwave oven for 1 to 2 minutes until hot and then serve.

Nutrition:

- **Calories:** 81;
- **Fats:** 6 g;
- **Protein:** 1 g;
- **Carb:** 2 g;
- **Fiber:** 0 g

Chapter 14. MAIN FOR EVENTS RECIPES-CHRISTMAS

162.   SAUTÉED CARROT AND GREEN ONIONS

Easy/Gluten-free/Vegan

Preparation time: 5 minutes;

Cooking time: 15 minutes;

Servings: 2

Ingredients:

- 4 carrots, peeled, sliced in rounds
- 2 green onions, diced
- ½ teaspoon salt
- ¾ tablespoon olive oil
- ½ tablespoon butter, unsalted

EXTRA:

- ¼ teaspoon ground black pepper

Directions:

1. Take a medium bowl, fill it half full with water, add some ice, and set aside until required.
2. Take a medium saucepan, place it over medium heat, fill it half full with water, add 2/3 teaspoon salt, stir until mixed and bring it to a rolling boil.
3. Then add carrot slices, cook them for 3 to 5 minutes, don't overcook, and then transfer them to the bowl containing ice-chilled water.
4. Let carrots soak until cooled and then pat dry.
5. Take a medium skillet pan, place it over medium heat, add oil and butter and wait until butter melts.
6. Then add carrot sliced and cook for 3 to 5 minutes per side until golden brown.
7. Add green onions, stir until mixed and cook for another minute.
8. Season carrots with salt and black pepper and serve.

Nutrition:

- **Calories:** 125;
- **Fats:** 8 g;
- **Protein:** 1 g;
- **Carb:** 11 g;
- **Fiber:** 3 g

163.   CHICKPEAS AND RICE

Easy/Gluten-free

Preparation time: 5 minutes

Cooking time: 15 minutes

Servings: 2

Ingredients:

- 1 tomato, chopped
- 6 ounces canned chickpeas, liquid reserved
- 10 ounces of brown rice
- 1 tablespoon olive oil
- 2/3 teaspoon salt

EXTRA:

- 1/3 teaspoon ground black pepper
- ½ teaspoon red pepper flakes
- ½ teaspoon cumin seeds
- Water as needed

Directions:

1. Take a medium skillet pan, add oil, and when hot, add tomatoes, stir and cook for 2 to 3 minutes until softened.
2. Then add salt, black pepper, red pepper, and cumin, stir until mixed and cook for 1 minute.
3. Pour reserved chickpea liquid in a cup and add water so that liquid is 1 2/3 cup.
4. Add chickpeas into the pan, stir until coated, cook for 1 minute, then pour in the liquid and bring it to a simmer.
5. Then add rice, switch heat to medium-low heat and cook for 4 to 5 minutes until water is absorbed by rice and rice have turned tender. When done, fluff rice with a fork and then serve.

Nutrition:

- **Calories:** 709;
- **Fats:** 31 g;
- **Protein:** 11 g;
- **Carb:** 13 g;
- **Fiber:** 2 g

164.   POTATOES AND MUSHROOMS

Easy/Gluten-free/Vegan

Preparation time: 5 minutes

Cooking time: 15 minutes

Servings: 2

Ingredients:

- 8 ounces diced potato
- 4 ounces sliced mushrooms
- ½ teaspoon garlic powder
- 1 tablespoon olive oil
- 3 tablespoons almond milk, unsweetened

EXTRA:

- ¼ teaspoon salt
- 1/8 teaspoon ground black pepper
- 2 tablespoons water

Directions:

1. Take a medium skillet pan, place it over medium heat, add oil and when hot, add mushrooms, stir in garlic powder and cook for 5 minutes.
2. Stir in water, then add potatoes, season with salt and black pepper, and continue cooking for 5 minutes or more until potatoes have cooked.
3. Switch heat to the low level, stir in milk, and then simmer for 5 to 7 minutes until vegetables have thoroughly cooked. Serve straight away.

Nutrition:

- **Calories:** 158;
- **Fats:** 8 g;
- **Protein:** 3 g;
- **Carb:** 5 g;
- **Fiber:** 11 g

165.   PARMESAN AND WINE TILAPIA

Easy/Gluten-free

Preparation time: 10 minutes

Cooking time: 15 minutes

Servings: 2

Ingredients:

- 1/4 cup all-purpose flour
- 1/2 cup grated Parmesan cheese
- 1/2 teaspoon dried thyme
- 1/2 teaspoon dried dill weed
- 1/4 teaspoon salt
- 1/2 cup milk
- 1/2 cup all-purpose flour
- 4 (4 oz.) tilapia fillets
- 2 tablespoons butter
- 1/4 cup dry white wine
- 1/4cup milk

Directions:

1. Get a bowl, combine salt, a quarter of a cup of flour, dill, parmesan, and thyme.
2. Get a 2nd bowl and add in 1/2 cup of flour.
3. Get the 3rd bowl and add in 1/2 a cup of milk.
4. Coat your fish with the contents of the 2nd bowl, then the 3rd bowl, and finally with the contents of the 1st bowl.
5. For 3 minutes, each side browns the tilapia in butter.
6. Now set the heat to low and cook everything for 4 more minutes. Then place the fish to the side.
7. Turn up the heat and add the first bowl (flour with spices) to the pan.
8. Pour in the wine and cook the mix for 7 minutes until it becomes sauce-like.
9. Slowly stir in a quarter of a cup of milk over low heat and cook everything for 3 more minutes.
10. Top your fish with the sauce.

Nutrition:

- **Calories:** 324 kcal
- **Fat:** 11.2 g
- **Carbohydrates:** 20.8g
- **Protein:** 30.8 g
- **Cholesterol:** 69 mg
- **Sodium:** 409 mg

166.   __EASY BAKED TILAPIA__

Easy/Gluten-free

Preparation time: 20 minutes

Cooking time: 20 minutes

Servings: 8

Ingredients:

- 1/2 cup of milk
- 1/2 cup prepared ranch dressing
- 1/2 cup all-purpose flour
- 1 cup dry bread crumbs
- 1/2 cup grated Parmesan cheese
- 1/2 teaspoon seasoned salt
- 1/2 teaspoon ground black pepper
- 1/2 teaspoon celery salt
- 1/2 teaspoon garlic powder
- 1/2 teaspoon onion powder
- 1/2 teaspoon ground paprika
- 1/2 teaspoon dried parsley
- 1/4 teaspoon dried basil
- Cooking spray
- 8 (6 oz.) tilapia fillets

Directions:

1. Set your oven to 425 degrees before doing anything else.
2. Cover a casserole dish with foil and then coat it with nonstick spray.
3. Get a bowl, combine milk and the dressing.
4. Get a 2nd bowl for your flour.
5. Get a 3rd bowl, combine: Parsley, bread crumbs, basil, parmesan, paprika, seasoned salt, onion powder, black pepper, and celery salt.
6. Now coat this mix with some nonstick spray until it is slightly moist. Then stir the mix a few times.
7. Do these 3 more times (spray then stir).
8. Now pour this mix in a plastic bag that can be resealed.
9. Coat your fish with the contents of the 2nd bowl, then the 1st bowl, and finally put each piece individually into your plastic bag and shake everything to coat the fish.

10. Place your fish pieces in the casserole dish and coat them with a little more cooking spray.

11. Cook everything in the oven for 23 minutes.

Nutrition:

- **Calories:** 357 kcal
- **Fat:** 12.8 g
- **Carbohydrates:** 17.8 g
- **Protein:** 39.8 g
- **Cholesterol:** 71 mg
- **Sodium:** 550 mg

167. BUTTER, GARLIC, AND TOMATOES TILAPIA

Easy/Gluten-free

Preparation time: 10 minutes

Cooking time: 15 minutes

Servings: 4

Ingredients:

- 4 (4 oz.) fillets tilapia
- Salt and pepper to taste
- 4 tablespoon butter
- 3 cloves garlic, pressed
- 4 fresh basil leaves, diced
- 1 large tomato, diced
- 1 cup white wine

Directions:

1. Get an outdoor grill hot and coat the grate with some oil before doing anything else.

2. Now lay all your pieces of fish on a big piece of foil.

3. Coat each piece with pepper and salt then put 1 tablespoon. of butter on each one.

4. Now top each piece with tomato, basil, and garlic then cover everything with the wine.

5. Wrap some foil around the fish and seal it tightly.

6. Place the foiled fish in a casserole dish and bring everything over to the grill.

7. Grill your fish for 17 minutes.

8. Enjoy.

Nutrition:

- **Calories:** 277 kcal

- **Fat:** 13.1 g
- **Carbohydrates:** 4.2g
- **Protein:** 23.7 g
- **Cholesterol:** 72 mg
- **Sodium:** 159 mg

---

168.   SPICY GARLIC TILAPIA

Easy/Gluten-free

Preparation time: 5 minutes

Cooking time: 30 minutes

Servings: 4

Ingredients:

- 4 (4 oz.) fillets tilapia
- 4 cloves crushed garlic
- 3 tablespoon Olive oil
- 1 onion, diced
- 1/4 teaspoon cayenne pepper

Directions:

1. Take your pieces of garlic and rub the pieces of fish with it. Now place everything into a casserole dish.
2. Coat your tilapia with olive oil and then layer your onions over everything.
3. Place a covering around the dish and place everything in the fridge for 8 hrs.
4. Set your oven to 350 degrees before doing anything else.
5. Top your fish with the cayenne and cook everything in the oven for 32 minutes.
6. Enjoy.

Nutrition:

- **Calories:** 217 kcal
- **Fat** 11.7 g
- **Carbohydrates** 3.6 g
- **Protein:** 23.5 g
- **Cholesterol:** 41 mg
- **Sodium:** 74 mg

169.   SALMON WITH BABY ARUGULA

Easy/Gluten-free

Preparation Time: 25 minutes

Cooking time: 10 minutes

Servings: 2

Ingredients:

- Salmon (2 center-cut filets)
- Olive oil (1 ½ tablespoon)
- Black pepper
- Lemon juice (1 ½ tablespoon)
- All-purpose seasoning (1/8 teaspoon)

FOR SALAD:

- Cherry tomatoes (2/3 cup, cut in half)
- Black pepper
- Wine vinegar (1 tablespoon)
- Baby arugula (3 cups)
- Red onion (1/4 cup, sliced)
- Olive oil (1 tablespoon, extra virgin)

Directions:

1. Season fish with all-purpose, oil, and lemon juice; marinate for 15 minutes.
2. Heat the skillet and place the salmon onto the skin side into the pot and cook for 3 minutes. Use a spatula to lift fish to avoid sticking lightly.
3. Lower heat and cover pan; cook for 4 minutes until skin is crispy.
4. Combine onion, tomatoes, and arugula in a bowl then drizzle with vinegar and oil.
5. Serve salad with fish.

Nutrition:

- **Calories:** 390
- **Carbs:** 4 g
- **Fat:** 23 g
- **Protein:** 40 g

Chapter 15. MAIN FOR EVENTS RECIPES-EASTER

170.   BAKED COD & GREEN BEANS

Easy/Gluten-free/Vegan

Preparation Time: 30 minutes

Cooking time: 15 minutes

Servings: 1

Ingredients:

- Olive oil (2 teaspoons)
- Cod (4 oz.)
- Green beans (2 cups)
- Blueberries (1/2 cup)
- Old-fashioned oats (1 tablespoon)
- Tomato (2 slices)

Directions:

1. Set oven to 400°F.
2. Combine oats and half of oil in a bowl and use the mixture to coat fish.
3. Coat baking tray with cooking spray and place fish onto tray and top with the tomato slices and bake for 15 minutes.
4. Steam green beans and serve with fish and blueberries.

Nutrition:

- **Calories:** 350
- **Carbs:** 39 g
- **Fat:** 11 g
- **Protein:** 27 g

171.   BAKED SCALLOPS

Easy/Gluten-free

Preparation Time: 30 minutes

Cooking time: 10 minutes

Servings: 1

Ingredients:

- Bay scallops (3 oz.)
- Oats (1 tablespoon, old-fashioned)

- Olive oil (1 ½ teaspoon, extra virgin)
- Lemon pepper
- Garbanzo beans (1/4 cup, low salt)
- Cucumber (1 cup)
- White wine (3 tablespoons)
- Cheddar cheese (1/2 oz., low fat, shredded)
- Lemon juice (3 tablespoons, freshly squeezed)
- Romaine lettuce (3 cups, chopped)
- Tomato (1)

Directions:

1. Put scallops into a container and cover with white wine; cover the container and put it into the refrigerator overnight.
2. Set oven to 350° F.
3. Remove scallops from wine and top with oats and cheese.
4. Place onto a baking tray and bake for 10 minutes.
5. Combine lemon pepper, lemon juice, and oil in a small bowl.
6. Mix together garbanzo beans, cucumber, lettuce, and tomato.
7. Serve salad topped with lemon dressing and baked scallops.

Nutrition:

- **Calories:** 358
- **Carbs**: 34 g
- **Fat:** 11 g
- **Protein:** 27 g

172. <u>**INDIAN INSPIRED FILET OF FISH**</u>

Medium/Gluten-free

Preparation time: 20 minutes

Cooking time: 35 minutes

Servings: 4

Ingredients:

MARINADE:

- 2 teaspoons Dijon mustard
- 1 teaspoon ground black pepper
- 1/2 teaspoon salt

- 2 tablespoons canola oil
- 4 white fish fillets
- 1 onion, coarsely chopped
- 4 cloves garlic, roughly chopped
- 1 (1 inch) piece fresh ginger root, peeled and chopped
- 5 cashew halves
- 1 tablespoon canola oil
- 2 teaspoons cayenne pepper, or to taste
- 1/2 teaspoon ground turmeric
- 1 teaspoon ground cumin
- 1 teaspoon ground coriander
- 1 teaspoon salt
- 1 teaspoon white sugar
- 1/2 cup chopped tomato
- 1/4 cup vegetable broth
- 1/4 cup chopped fresh cilantro

Directions

1. Set your oven at 350 degrees F before doing anything else.
2. Coat fish fillets with a mixture of mustard, pepper, 1/2 teaspoon salt, and 2 tablespoons of canola oil before refrigerating it for 30 minutes.
3. Cook blended mixture of onion, cashews, ginger, and garlic for two minutes before adding cayenne pepper, 1 teaspoon salt, turmeric, cumin, coriander, and sugar in the pan, and cooking it for 5 more minutes.
4. Add chopped tomato and vegetable broth before pouring it over the fish in the baking dish.
5. Bake this in the preheated oven for about 30 minutes.
6. Sprinkle some chopped cilantro for garnishing.

Nutrition:

- **Calories:** 338 kcal
- **Cholesterol:** 56 mg
- **Fat:** 13.5 g
- **Fiber:** 2.3 g
- **Protein:** 41.6 g
- **Sodium:** 2715 mg

173. APPLE SCALLOPS

Easy/Gluten-free

Preparation Time: 15 minutes

Cooking time: 5 minutes

Servings: 1

Ingredients:

- Celery (3/4 cup, diced)
- Vegetable broth (1/2 cup, no salt)
- Ginger (1/2 teaspoon, grated)
- Cardamom (1 teaspoon)
- Olive oil (1 teaspoon)
- Carrot (1/3 cup, shredded)
- Green beans (1 cup)
- Green apple (3/4, without core and chopped)
- Scallops (4 oz.)
- Walnuts (1 tablespoon, crushed)

Directions:

1. Add carrots and celery to the pot along with 3 tablespoon broth and cook for 5 minutes.
2. Put in the leftover broth along with ginger, cardamom, green beans, and apple; mix together to combine and cook until thoroughly heated.
3. Heat skillet and coat with cooking spray and cook scallops on all sides until golden.
4. Serve with vegetables and top with walnuts and olive oil.

Nutrition:

- **Calories:** 324
- **Carbs:** 36 g
- **Fat:** 11 g
- **Protein:** 23 g

---

174. EASY LITTLE FISH TACOS

Easy/Gluten-free

Preparation time: 20 minutes

Cooking time: 30 minutes

Servings: 8

Ingredients:

- 1pound shark fillets
- 12 (6 inches) corn tortillas
- 1/4 cup canola oil
- 1/4 cup lemon juice
- 1 clove garlic, minced
- 1 teaspoon dried oregano
- 1 teaspoon Cajun seasoning
- 1 cup shredded Cheddar cheese
- 2 quarts' vegetable oil for frying

Directions:

1. Coat shark strips with a mixture of canola oil, oregano, lemon juice, garlic, and Cajun-style spice mix, and marinate it for at least an hour before placing each one of them on microwaved tortillas.
2. Fold it up and seal it up with a toothpick before frying it up for 4 minutes.
3. Place all these tortillas on the baking dish and bake at 350 degrees F for five minutes.
4. Serve.

Nutrition:

- **Calories:** 642 kcal
- **Cholesterol:** 55 mg
- **Fat:** 51.3 g
- **Fiber:** 3.5 g
- **Protein:** 22.4 g
- **Sodium:** 295 mg

175.   **EASY DEEP-FRIED SNAPPER**

Easy/Gluten-free

Preparation time: 5 minutes

Cooking time: 10 minutes

Servings: 4

Ingredients:

- 1quart vegetable oil for frying
- 1 lb. red snapper fillets
- 1 egg, beaten
- 1/2 cup dry bread crumbs

Directions:

1. Dip fish fillets in beaten egg before dipping in the bread crumbs.

2. Fry these fillets in hot oil until you see that it is golden brown.

3. Serve.

Nutrition:

- **Calories:** 386 kcal
- **Cholesterol:** 92 mg
- **Fat:** 26.2 g
- **Fiber:** 0.6 g
- **Protein:** 26.8 g
- **Sodium:** 175 mg

176. LOUISIANA STYLE MAHI MAHI

Easy/Gluten-free/Vegan

Preparation time: 10 minutes

Cooking time: 20 minutes

Servings: 2

Ingredients:

- 2 (4 oz.) fillets Mahi Mahi
- 2 teaspoons olive oil
- 1/2 cup salted butter
- 1 clove garlic, minced
- 1 tablespoon lemon juice
- 2 drops Louisiana style hot sauce, or to taste
- 1 Roma tomato, seeded and chopped (optional)
- 1 green onion, chopped

Directions:

1. Set your oven at 450 degrees F before doing anything else.

2. Coat mahi-mahi fillets with olive oil and places them in the baking dish

3. Bake this in the preheated oven for about 20 minutes.

4. Cook garlic, lemon juice, and hot sauce in hot butter for one minute before adding tomato and green onion.

5. Continue cooking for another 3 minutes before pouring it over the baked fish.

Nutrition:

- **Calories:** 556 kcal
- **Cholesterol:** 204 mg
- **Fat:** 51.7 g
- **Fiber:** 0.6 g
- **Protein:** 21.7 g
- **Sodium:** 452 mg

177. ORZO AND SPICED SHRIMP

Easy/Gluten-free

Preparation Time: 40 minutes

Cooking time: 10 minutes

Servings: 2

Ingredients:

- Orzo pasta (2/3 cup)
- Olive oil (1 tablespoon)
- Black pepper
- Chile powder (1/2 teaspoon, ancho)
- Cumin (1/4 teaspoon)
- Cayenne pepper
- Lime juice (3 tablespoons, freshly squeezed)
- Red onion (1/2, sliced)
- Basil leaves (2 tablespoons)
- Smoked paprika (1 teaspoon)
- Agave nectar (1 teaspoon)
- Coriander (1/4 teaspoon)
- Jumbo shrimp (3 oz., deveined and without shell)
- Lettuce (8 leaves)
- Tomatoes (2, sliced)

Directions:

1. Put oil and basil into a processor or blender and pulse until smooth. Add black pepper and lime juice, mix together and put aside until needed.

2. Heat grill.

3. Combine chili powder, cumin, cayenne pepper, paprika, sugar, and coriander in a small bowl.

4. Coat shrimp with cooking spray and spice blend and put aside; prepare orzo as directed on package, run under cold water and drain.

5. Pour lime juice over orzo.

6. Grill shrimp for 4 minutes until slightly charred.

7. Place lettuce on a place and top with orzo, onion, and tomato and drizzle with basil blend.

8. Add shrimp and serve.

Nutrition:

- **Calories:** 345
- **Carbs:** 35 g
- **Fat:** 11 g
- **Protein:** 26 g

---

178.   INDIAN STYLE TANDOORI CATFISH

Easy/Gluten-free

Preparation time: 10 minutes

Cooking time: 17 minutes

Servings: 6

Ingredients:

- 1/3 cup vinegar
- 4 cloves garlic
- 1 tablespoon chopped fresh ginger
- 1/2 teaspoon salt
- 1 tablespoon cayenne pepper
- 1 tablespoon ground coriander
- 1 tablespoon ground cumin
- 1/2 cup vegetable oil
- 2 lbs. thick catfish fillets, cut into large chunks

Directions:

1. Coat fish chunks with a mixture of vinegar, cayenne, garlic, ginger, salt, coriander, cumin, and oil before marinating it for at least four hours.
2. Heat the broiler.
3. Now broil the fish in the preheated broiler for about 10 minutes before turning and brushing it with the reserved marinade.
4. Broil for another 7 minutes.
5. Serve.

Nutrition:

- **Calories:** 272 kcal
- **Cholesterol:** 71 mg
- **Fat:** 30.2 g
- **Fiber:** 0.9 g
- **Protein:** 24.1 g
- **Sodium:** 277 mg

179.   EASY JALAPENO GARLIC TROUT

Easy/Gluten-free/Vegan

Preparation time: 10 minutes

Cooking time: 20 minutes

Servings: 2

Ingredients:

- 2 rainbow trout fillets
- 1 tablespoon olive oil
- 2 teaspoon garlic salt
- 1 teaspoon ground black pepper
- 1 fresh jalapeno pepper, sliced
- 1 lemon, sliced

Directions:

1. Set your oven at 400 degrees F° before doing anything else.
2. Coat fillets with olive oil, black pepper, and garlic salt before putting jalapeno slices, lemon juice, and lemon slices over fillets in some aluminum foil.
3. Wrap these foils up before placing them in a baking dish.
4. Bake in the preheated oven for about 20 minutes.

Nutrition:

- **Calories:** 213 kcal
- **Cholesterol:** 67 mg
- **Fat:** 10.9 g
- **Fiber:** 3 g
- **Protein:** 24.3 g
- **Sodium:** 1850 mg

180.   VERACRUZ SCALLOPS WITH GREEN CHILE SAUCE

Easy/Gluten-free/Vegan

Preparation time: 20 minutes

Cooking Time: 20 minutes

Servings: 8 persons

Ingredients:

- 24 (2 ounces) sea scallops, large pieces
- Finely grated juice and zest of 1 lime, fresh
- Vegetable oil, as required

FOR RUB:

- 1 teaspoon pure chili powder
- ½ teaspoon ground cumin
- 1 teaspoon paprika
- ½ teaspoon oregano, dried
- 1 teaspoon kosher salt
- ¼ teaspoon freshly ground black pepper

FOR SAUCE:

- 3 long Anaheim chili peppers
- ½ cup sour cream
- 3 scallions (green and white parts only), coarsely chopped
- ½ cup mayonnaise
- 1 garlic clove, small
- ¼ cup fresh cilantro leaves & tender stems; loosely packed
- Finely grated juice & zest of 1 lime, fresh
- ¼ teaspoon kosher salt

Directions:

1. Preheat the grill over high heat for direct cooking

2. Grill the chili peppers for a couple of minutes, until turn blackened & blistered in spots, with the lid open, turning every now and then. Remove the chili from grill; set aside until easy to handle. Once done, remove the stem ends & discard. Scrape off & discard the blackened skins using a sharp knife. Coarsely chop the leftover parts of chili & drop them into a blender or food processor. Add the scallions followed by garlic and cilantro. A process on high power until you get a coarse paste-like consistency, scraping down the sides of your bowl as required. Add the leftover sauce ingredients & process on high power again until you get a smooth sauce.

3. Next, mix the entire rub ingredients together in a small-sized mixing bowl.

4. Rinse the scallops under cold, running tap water & remove the tough, small muscle. Place the cleaned scallops in a large-sized mixing bowl & add oil (enough to coat). Add the rub mixture followed by the lime juice and lime zest. Mix well until the scallops are evenly coated.

5. Grill the scallops for 4 to 6 minutes, until opaque in the middle and firm slightly on the surface, with the lid closed, turning once. Remove from the grill; serve warm with the prepared sauce and enjoy.

Nutrition:

- **Calories:** 208;
- **Fats:** 8 g;
- **Protein:** 3 g;
- **Carb:** 5 g;
- **Fiber:** 2 g

181.   **GRILLED FRESH FISH**

Easy/Gluten-free

Preparation Time: 10 Minutes

Cooking Time: 25 Minutes

Servings: 4 Persons

Ingredients:

- 1 whole firm white fish fillet: such as halibut, sea bass, or cod
- 2 whole lemons; sliced into half
- Traeger Fin & Feather Rub, as required

Directions:

1. Preheat your wood pellet to 325 F° in advance for 12 to 15 minutes, lid closed.

2. Season the fish with Rub & let sit for half an hour.

3. Place the fish & lemons directly over the hot grill grates, cut side down. Cook until the fish is flaky, for 12 to 15 minutes. Ensure that you don't overcook the fish. Serve immediately with grilled lemons and enjoy.

Nutrition:

- **Calories:** 115;
- **Fats:** 8 g;
- **Protein:** 3 g;
- **Carb:** 5 g;
- **Fiber:** 2 g

182. SANIBEL SOUTHERN STYLE

Easy/Gluten-free/Vegan

Preparation Time: 10 minutes

Cooking time: 15

Servings: 4

Ingredients:

- 1 tablespoon. olive oil
- Salt and pepper to taste
- 2 (8 oz.) steaks halibut
- 3 tablespoons capers, with liquid
- 1/2 cup white wine
- 1 teaspoon chopped garlic
- 1/4 cup butter

Directions:

1. Heat the olive oil on medium-high heat and fry the halibut steaks in a large skillet, till browned from all sides.
2. Transfer the steaks into a bowl and keep aside.
3. In the same pan, add the wine and with a spatula scrape any browned bits from the bottom.

4. Cook till the wine is almost absorbed.

5. Stir in the garlic, butter, capers, salt, and pepper, and simmer for 1 minute.

6. Stir in the steaks and cook till the fish flakes easily with a fork.

Nutrition:

- **Calories:** 284 kcal
- **Fat:** 17 g
- **Protein:** 24.2 g
- **Cholesterol:** 72 mg
- **Sodium:** 337

183.   **HALIBUT**

Easy/Gluten-free/Vegan

Preparation Time: 10 minutes

Cooking time: 25 minutes

Servings: 4

Ingredients:

- 2 lbs. halibut steak, 1 1/2inch thickness
- 1/4 teaspoon ground white pepper
- 1 cup sour cream
- 1 pinch dried dill weed
- 1/2 cup chopped green onions
- 1/3 cup grated Parmesan cheese
- 2 tablespoons. Butter softened
- 1/2 teaspoon salt

Directions:

1. Before doing anything else, set your oven to 350 degrees F and grease a 13x9inch baking dish with the butter.

2. Arrange the halibut steak in the prepared baking dish.

3. In a bowl, mix together the sour cream, green onions, butter, salt, white pepper, and dill.

4. Place the sour cream mixture over the halibut steak evenly. Cook in the oven for about 2025 minutes.

5. Bring out the halibut from the oven and sprinkle with the Parmesan cheese.

6. Now, set your oven to broiler and arrange the oven rack about 6inches from the heating element.

7. Cook the fish under the broiler for about 23 minutes.

Nutrition:

- **Calories:** 461 kcal
- **Fat:** 24 g
- **Protein:** 53.3 g
- **Cholesterol:** 131 mg
- **Sodium:** 593 mg

184.   RESTAURANT STYLE HALIBUT

Medium/Gluten-free/Vegan

Preparation Time: 15 minutes

Cooking time: 35 minutes

Servings: 6

Ingredients:

- 2 lbs. halibut fillets
- 1 (16 oz.) can diced tomatoes
- Salt and pepper to taste
- 2 tablespoons capers
- 1/4 cup olive oil
- 4 cloves garlic, minced
- 1/2 cup chopped fresh parsley
- 1 yellow onion, thinly sliced
- 2 stalks celery, chopped
- 1 green bell pepper, chopped

Directions:

1. Before doing anything else, set your oven to 475 degrees F and lightly grease a 13x9inch baking dish.
2. Wash the halibut and pat dry with the paper towels.

3. Cut the halibut into serving size pieces 4. Arrange the halibut pieces into a prepared baking dish and sprinkle with the salt and pepper.

4. Mix together the olive oil, parsley, onion, celery, bell pepper, tomatoes, capers, and garlic in a bowl.

5. Place the oil mixture over the halibut pieces evenly.

6. Cook in the oven for about 20 minutes.

7. Remove from the oven and keep aside for about 10 minutes before serving.

Nutrition:

- **Calories:** 291 kcal
- **Fat:** 12 g
- **Protein:** 34 g
- **Cholesterol:** 56 mg
- **Sodium** 304 mg

185.   **WHANGAREI STYLE**

Medium/Gluten-free

Preparation Time: 20 minutes

Cooking time: 25 minutes

Servings: 4

Ingredients:

- 1 tablespoon. butter
- 1/2 teaspoon red pepper flakes
- 1 tablespoon. olive oil
- 1 lb. mussels, cleaned and debearded
- 2 tablespoons minced garlic
- 1 cup chopped green onions
- 2 tablespoons minced shallots
- 1 tablespoon. capers
- 3 cups canned tomato sauce
- 1 tablespoon. Italian seasoning

Directions:

1. Heat the oil and butter on the medium temperature in a skillet and sauté the shallots, garlic, and capers for about 5 minutes.

2. Stir in the Italian herbs, tomato sauce, and red pepper flakes and reduce the heat to medium-low.

3. Simmer, covered for about 10 minutes.

4. Stir in the mussels and increase the heat to medium-high.

5. Cook, covered for about 10 minutes.

6. Discard any unopened mussels from the skillet.

7. Serve with a garnishing of the green onions.

Nutrition:

- **Calories:** 142 kcal
- **Fat:** 7.1 g
- **Carbohydrates:** 15.8g
- **Protein:** 6.9 g
- **Cholesterol:** 17 mg
- **Sodium:** 1102 mg

186. CIOPPINO

Medium/Gluten-free

Preparation Time: 20 minutes

Cooking time: 25 minutes

Servings: 4

Ingredients:

- 1 ounce can of whole San Marzano plum tomatoes in juice (you can also use an equal amount of stewed tomatoes, crushed tomatoes, or diced tomatoes in the juice)
- 2 cups bottled fish broth or clam juice
- 5 tablespoons of olive oil
- 1 large yellow onion, chopped
- 5 garlic cloves, minced
- 2 tablespoons of tomato paste
- 1 teaspoon dried oregano
- 2 sprigs of fresh thyme
- 2 bay leaves
- 1 teaspoon crushed red pepper flakes
- 1 1/2 cups of dry white wine
- 1 pound large shrimp, uncooked, peeled, and deveined
- 1 pound Manila or small necked clams in the shell, scrubbed
- 1 pound mussels in the shell, scrubbed and bound
- Large 3/4 pound scallops, sturdy adductor muscles trimmed from the sides if needed

- 1 1/2pound firm white fish such as halibut, snapper, cod, or sea bass (or a mixture thereof), skinned, boned, and cut into 2inch pieces
- 3 tablespoons chopped fresh basil (optional)
- 1/4 cup chopped fresh flatleaf Italian parsley
- Kosher salt, to taste
- Freshly ground black pepper, to taste

Directions:

1. Heat a large heavy bottom pot over medium-high heat, then add the olive oil and let it warm for another 30 seconds or so until it is hot but not steaming. Add onions and a pinch of salt and sauté for about 5 minutes or until onions are soft and translucent. Add garlic and sauté, stirring, for another minute. Don't let the garlic brown.

2. Add tomato paste and sauté for another minute, stirring all the time. Add oregano, thyme, bay leaves, and crushed red pepper, then add white wine and stir to combine. Boil over low heat until the wine is halved, about four minutes. Add the tomatoes and their juice, along with the fish stock or clam juice, and stir to combine. If you use whole or crushed tomatoes, use a wooden spoon to break them into smaller pieces. Bring the liquid back to a simmer and cook for about 30 minutes, but do not allow to boil.

3. When the broth flavors have come together, add the clams and mussels to the pot and cover; cook for about 5 minutes, then add shrimp, scallops, and fish, and simmer for another 5 minutes, or until seafood is well cooked.

4. Discard any unopened clams and mussels. Taste the broth and season with salt and pepper as needed. Discard the bay leaves and thyme sprigs and add the fresh basil if you use it, then serve the soup right away, dividing the different types of seafood between the bowls and garnishing each with parsley.

Nutrition:

- **Calories:** 162 kcal
- **Fat:** 7.1 g
- **Protein:** 5.9 g
- **Cholesterol:** 17 mg
- **Sodium:** 1402 mg

187.   **BAKED EASY FISH ON PARCHMENT**

Easy/Gluten-free/Vegan

Preparation Time: 20 minutes

Cooking time: 20 minutes

Servings: 4

Ingredients:

- 1 firm meat white fish fillet (6 ounces), such as halibut, cod, or haddock (fillet should be 3/4 to 1 1/4 inches thick)
- 1 tablespoon of extra virgin olive oil
- Salt
- Freshly ground black pepper
- 1 bay leaf, cut in half (optional)
- Fresh herbs, such as chives, parsley, tarragon, or chervil (optional)
- 1 tablespoon unsalted butter
- 3 thin lemon slices
- 1 tablespoon of dry white wine or water

Directions:

1. Heat oven to 400 ° F and place a rack in the middle.
2. Draw a large piece of parchment paper (about 17 by 11 inches) and, with one of the closest longer edges, fold it in half from left to right. Using scissors, cut a large heart shape.
3. Place the fish in the center of the middle of the parchment heart. (The heart should be large enough that there is at least an 11 / 2inch border around the fillet.)
4. Place the parchment heart on a baking sheet. Drizzle the fish with half the olive oil, rub the oil all over the fillet, and season with salt and pepper.
5. Place half of the bay leaf and a few sprigs of herbs (if used) over the fish. Break the butter into small pieces and place them on the herbs.
6. Place the lemon slices on everything and drizzle with the remaining oil.
7. Fold the parchment heart to cover the fish. (The edges of the heart should be aligned.) Starting at the rounded end, bring the edges together, folding them over on themselves and leaving the last two inches unfolded at the pointed end. Tilt the package up slightly and pour in the wine or water. Finish crimping the edges, then twist the pointed end once and fold the "tail" underneath.
8. Place the baking sheet in the oven and bake for 10 minutes for a 3/4inch thick fillet or 12 minutes for a 1 to 11 / 4inch thick fillet.
9. Remove the baking sheet from the oven and transfer the parchment pack to a plate. Serve immediately, cutting on the parchment table with scissors or a knife.

Nutrition:

- **Calories:** 122 kcal
- **Fat:** 7.1 g
- **Protein:** 6.9 g

- **Cholesterol:** 17 mg
- **Sodium:** 1102 mg

188. <u>FRENCH MUSSELS</u>

Easy/Gluten-free/Vegan

Preparation Time: 20 minutes

Cooking time: 20 minutes

Servings: 4

Ingredients:

- 2 tablespoons butter
- 20 fresh basil leaves, torn
- 3 tablespoons minced garlic
- 2 cups white wine
- 4 shallots, chopped
- 1 tablespoon. cornstarch
- 4 cups beef broth
- 1/2 cup light cream
- 1 jalapeno pepper, minced
- 5 lbs. fresh mussels, scrubbed and
- 1 red chili pepper, minced
- Debearded
- 4 fresh tomatoes, coarsely chopped

Directions:

1. Melt the butter on the medium temperature in a large soup pan, and sauté the shallots and garlic till browned lightly.
2. Add the red chili pepper, jalapeño, and a splash of the broth and simmer for a few minutes.
3. Stir in the remaining broth, white wine, tomatoes, and basil and bring to a boil.
4. Meanwhile, in a bowl, mix together the cornstarch and a little amount of the light cream.
5. In the pan, add the remaining light cream and cornstarch mixture and bring to a boil.
6. Cook for about 5 minutes.

Nutrition:

- **Calories:** 413 kcal
- **Fat:** 13.8 g
- **Carbohydrates:** 27.2g

- **Protein:** 24 g
- **Cholesterol:** 80 mg
- **Sodium:** 1109 mg

189.   STEAMED SEA BASS IN BANANA LEAF WITH MINT AND COCONUT CHUTNEY

Easy/Gluten-free/Vegan

Preparation Time: 10 minutes

Cooking time: 30 minutes

Servings: 4

Ingredients:

- 1/2 cup coconut, grated, fresh or frozen
- 1 teaspoon of ginger garlic paste
- 1 teaspoon finely chopped fresh Thai green chili
- 1/2 teaspoon of cumin seeds
- 1/2 teaspoon ground turmeric
- 1/3 cup of fresh lemon juice
- 1/4 cup packaged mint leaves, cut into large chunks
- 1/2 cup coarsely chopped coriander, including stems
- 3/4 teaspoon of salt
- 1 spoon of sugar

FOR THE FISH:

- 4 sea bass fillets (3 1/2 to 4 ounces each), skinless and boneless
- 1/4 teaspoon ground turmeric
- 1/4 teaspoon of salt
- 2 teaspoons of fresh lemon juice
- 4 banana leaves, about 9 square inches
- 1/2 cup canola oil

Directions:

To make the hot sauce:

1. In a Nutri Bullet or small blender, combine the coconut, ginger garlic paste, green chili, cumin seeds, turmeric, and lemon juice. Blend for 3 minutes, shaking the bottle or scraping it from time to time, to

make a thick and fairly smooth puree. Add mint leaves and puree until smooth. Add the coriander, salt, and sugar and puree until smooth.

To make the fish:

1. In a medium bowl, cover the sea bass fillets with turmeric, salt, and lemon juice.

2. Microwave 2 of the banana leaves for 15 seconds to soften them and put them on a large cutting board. Place a fish fillet on the bottom half of each sheet. Spread 1 1/2 tablespoons of chutney over each fillet, then flip over and spread another 11/2 tablespoons of chutney on the other sides of the fillets. Fold the leaves in half over the fillets. Starting and ending at the fold, use a sharp knife to trim each pack, leaving a 1inch border around the fish on three sides. Transfer the packages to a baking sheet. Repeat with the remaining 2 banana leaves, the sea bass fillets, and the hot sauce. Refrigerate containers for 1 hour.

3. Preheat oven to 200° F. Has another large baking sheet ready.

4. In a large skillet, heat 1/4 cup of the oil over medium-high heat until it shines. Reduce the heat to medium and place two packages of fish in the pan next to each other. Cook for 3 minutes on each side. Transfer the packages to the baking sheet and put them in the oven to keep them warm. Clean the pan with a wad of paper towels and repeat with the rest of 1/4 cup of oil and two packages of fish. Serve immediately.

Nutrition:

- **Calories:** 122 kcal
- **Fat:** 7.1 g
- **Protein:** 6.9 g
- **Cholesterol:** 17 mg
- **Sodium:** 1102 mg

190.   **FISH AND FRENCH FRIES**

Easy/Gluten-free

Preparation Time: 20 minutes

Cooking time: 20 minutes

Servings: 4

Ingredients:

FOR THE FISH:

- 1 1/3 cups all-purpose flour
- 2 teaspoons of baking powder
- 1 teaspoon of kosher salt
- 1/4 teaspoon cayenne pepper

- 1/4 teaspoon garlic powder
- 1 bottle of cold beer
- About 6 cups of vegetable oil, for frying
- 1 pound firm meat white fish (such as pollock or cod), cut into 1inchlong strips
- About 1/2 cup cornstarch, for dredging

AT YOUR SERVICE:

- British style tabs (recipe link in the introduction)
- Malt vinegar
- Dijon tartar sauce (recipe link in the introduction)

Directions:

1. In a bowl, mix the flour, baking powder, half the salt, cayenne pepper, and garlic powder. Beat the beer until the dough is completely smooth and smooth. Refrigerate for at least 15 minutes and up to 1 hour ahead.

2. Heat 3 inches of vegetable oil in a large heavy-bottomed pot until it reaches 350 ° F on a frying thermometer. Prepare a baking rack placed on a rimmed baking sheet; set aside.

3. Lightly dredge the fish strips in cornstarch. Working in small batches, dip the fish into the batter so that it is evenly covered and immediately place it in the hot oil.

4. Cook, frequently turning, until golden, about 3 minutes. Use a slotted spoon to transfer pieces of fish to the prepared rack. Serve with British style fries, malt vinegar, and Dijon tartar sauce.

Nutrition:

Calories: 189 kcal

Fat: 7.1 g

Protein: 6.9 g

Cholesterol: 17 mg

Sodium: 302 mg

191.   __EASY FISH TACOS__

Easy/Gluten-free

Preparation Time: 15 minutes

Cooking time: 20 minutes

Servings: 4

Ingredients:

- 1 pound of firm white fish, such as tilapia, snapper, cod, mahimahi, or catfish
- 2 medium files, cut in half
- 1 medium garlic clove, finely minced
- 1/4 teaspoon ground cumin
- 1/4 teaspoon chili powder
- 2 tablespoons vegetable oil, plus more to grease the grills
- Kosher salt
- Freshly ground black pepper
- 1/2 small head of green or red cabbage (about 14 ounces), cored and thinly sliced
- 1/2 medium red onion, thinly sliced
- 1/4 cup coarsely chopped fresh cilantro
- 6 to 8 soft corn tortillas (6 inches)
- Avocado, sliced, for garnish (optional)
- Guacamole, to decorate (optional, see above)
- Sauce, to decorate (optional, see above)
- Sour cream, to decorate (optional)
- Hot sauce, to garnish (optional)

Directions:

1. Place the fish in a baking dish and squeeze a half a lime over it. Add garlic, cumin, chili powder, and 1 tablespoon of oil. Season with salt and pepper and rotate the fish in the marinade until it is evenly coated. Refrigerate and marinate for at least 15 minutes. Meanwhile, make the cabbage salad and heat the tortillas.

2. Combine cabbage, onion, and cilantro in a large bowl and squeeze half of a lime over it. Drizzle with remaining 1 tablespoon oil, season with salt and pepper and mix to combine. Taste and add more salt and pepper if necessary; set aside.

3. Heat tortillas by heating a medium skillet over medium-high heat. Add 1 tortilla at a time, turning to heat both sides, about 5minutes total. Wrap the hot tortillas in a clean kitchen towel and set aside while preparing the fish.

4. Brush the racks of a grill pan or outside pan with oil and heat over medium-high heat until hot. Remove the fish from the marinade and place it on the grill.

5. Cook without moving until the bottom of the fish has grill marks and is white and opaque at the bottom, about 3 minutes. Flip and grill the other side until white and opaque, about 2 to 3 minutes more. (It's okay if it breaks while flipping.) Transfer the fish to a plate.

6. Try the salad again and season as necessary with more lemon juice. Cut the remaining lime halves into wedges and serve with the tacos. To build a taco, tear up some of the cooked fish, place it on a warm tortilla, and top it with cabbage salad and any optional side dishes.

Nutrition:

- **Calories:** 282 kcal
- **Fat:** 7.1 g
- **Protein:** 6.9 g
- **Cholesterol:** 12 mg
- **Sodium:** 702 mg

192.   **FISH CAKE**

Easy/Gluten-free

Preparation Time: 10 minutes

Cooking time: 20 minutes

Servings: 4

Ingredients:

FOR THE MASH:

- 2 1/2 pounds Yukon Gold potatoes, peeled and quartered if large, halved if small
- 2 tablespoons kosher salt, more to taste
- 4 tablespoons unsalted butter (1/2 stick)
- 1/2 cup whole milk, heated, and more if needed
- Freshly ground black pepper, to taste

FOR FILLING:

- 6 tablespoons unsalted butter (3/4 stick), at room temperature
- 1 medium yellow onion, finely chopped
- 1 small carrot, finely chopped
- 1/3 cup all-purpose flour
- 3 cups whole milk
- 1/4 cup finely chopped flatleaf parsley
- 2 tablespoons chopped chives
- Kosher salt, to taste

- Freshly ground black pepper, to taste
- 1/2pound hot smoked salmon, peeled, boned, and broken into small pieces
- 1 1/2pound white fish fillets, such as halibut or cod, peeled, boned, and cut into small pieces

Directions:

To make the puree:

1. Place the potatoes in a saucepan and add cold water to cover by 2 inches. Add the measured salt and bring to a boil over high heat. Reduce heat to low and cook, occasionally stirring, until tender, about 20 minutes. Drain the potatoes well and return to the same pan in which they were cooked.

2. Add butter and milk and puree with a potato masher (or use a richer one). Add additional milk to make the creamy puree, but make sure it stays thick. Season to taste with extra salt, if necessary, and black pepper. Cover with lid and set aside.

To make the filling and bake:

1. Heat oven to 400 ° F and place a rack in the middle. In a saucepan over medium heat, melt 4 tablespoons of butter. Add the onion and carrot and cook until golden and tender, about 5 minutes.

2. Add the flour and beat to combine.

3. Slowly add milk, stirring well as you add to avoid lumps. Let the sauce simmer for a few minutes, then add the parsley and chives. Remove from the heat and season to taste with salt and pepper. Gently add the smoked and whitefish.

4. Place the mixture in a greased 2quart baking sheet.

5. Cover with tablespoons mashed potatoes reserved extending the puree in a uniform layer fish mixture. Rake the top with the tines of a fork to create a rough texture and tap with the remaining 2 tablespoons of butter.

6. Bake until bubbly and top is nice and brown, about 30 minutes.

Nutrition:

- **Calories:** 90.1 kcal
- **Fat:** 0 g
- **Protein:** 10 g
- **Carbs:** 10 g
- **Sodium:** 338 mg

193. CHARLES PHANS STEAMED PORK WITH SALTED FISH

Medium/Gluten-free

Preparation Time: 20 minutes

Cooking time: 40 minutes

Servings: 4

Ingredients:

- 1/2pound boneless pork ribs or ground pork
- 3 medium shiitake mushrooms, clean, destemmed, and finely chopped
- 1 medium shallot, finely chopped
- 1 tablespoon of fish sauce, plus more as needed
- 2 teaspoons cornstarch
- 1 teaspoon of olive oil, and more to drizzle
- Salt
- Freshly ground black pepper
- 1 piece of salted mackerel (2 by 1inch long and 1/2inch thick) or 5 anchovy fillets
- 1 (1inch) piece fresh ginger, peeled, thinly sliced, then cut into excellent matches
- Basic steamed white rice, to serve

Directions:

1. Fill a large wok with 1 inch of water and place a large bamboo steamer inside. (The water must not touch the bottom of the vaporizer

2. In the meantime, if you use pork ribs, cut the meat with a knife or knife until it is excellent and looks like a cake.

3. Place the pork (minced or ground) in a medium bowl. Add the mushrooms, shallots, fish sauce, cornstarch, oil, and a large pinch of salt and pepper and stir to combine. Check the mixture for proper dressing by forming a small, thin patty. Fry it until the center is no longer pink. Test by adding additional fish sauce, salt, or pepper as needed, keeping in mind that there will be more salt in the salted fish dish.

4. Place the pork mixture on a heat resistant plate with a slightly (to contain the juices) rim about 8 inches in diameter. Press the pork onto the plate to form a large 1/4inch thick patty. If you use salted mackerel, place it in the center of the pork patty. If you use anchovies, spread them in a single layer on top of the pork patty. Sprinkle evenly with ginger and drizzle with a little olive oil. Carefully place the plate in the bamboo steamer or on top of the aluminum coils. Cover the wok or skillet with an airtight lid or a sheet of aluminum foil and steam until the mixture is cooked through, about 8 to 10 minutes. Serve with rice.

Nutrition:

- **Calories:** 212 kcal
- **Fat:** 4.1 g
- **Protein:** 6.9 g
- **Cholesterol:** 17 mg

- **Sodium:** 312 mg

194.   STEAMED FISH WITH CHICKPEAS AND CURRANTS

Easy/Gluten-free

Preparation Time: 20 minutes

Cooking time: 20 minutes

Servings: 4

Ingredients:

- 1/4 cup plus 1 tablespoon of olive oil
- 1 teaspoon of ground cumin
- 1/2 teaspoon ground cinnamon
- 1/8 teaspoon ground sumac
- 4 (6 ounces) soft white meat fish fillets, such as Pacific halibut, grouper, cod, or haddock (fillets should be 3/4 inch to 1 1/4 inch thick)
- Kosher salt
- Freshly ground black pepper
- 1 medium yellow onion, diced
- 1 small fennel bulb, outer shell discarded, core removed and diced
- 1/2 cup dry white wine
- 2 tablespoons of currants
- 1 can (15 ounces) chickpeas, also known as chickpeas, drained and rinsed (about 1 1/2 cups)
- 1 cup bottled clam juice
- 1/4 cup coarsely chopped green olives
- 3 tablespoons finely chopped fresh coriander
- 2 tablespoons canned lemon, finely chopped
- 12 skinny slices of canned lemon

Directions:

1. Place a large, straight-sided skillet with an airtight lid on medium-high heat until hot. Add 1/4 cup oil, cumin, cinnamon, and sumac and cook, stirring, until aromatic, about 30 to 60 seconds. Remove the pan from the heat and immediately transfer half of the oil mixture to a large, shallow dish. Cool slightly.

2. Season the fish fillets with salt and pepper, transfer to the shallow dish, and rotate to coat with the spiced oil. Cover and refrigerate for 30 minutes.

3. Meanwhile, return skillet with remaining spiced oil over medium-high heat. Add onion and fennel, season with salt and pepper, and cook, stirring frequently, and lower heat if necessary until onion is translucent

about 5 minutes. Add the wine and raisins and cook over medium heat until the wine is almost evaporated about 3 to 4 minutes. Add the chickpeas, clam juice, olives, 2 tablespoons coriander, and the preserved chopped lemon and simmer. Cook until liquid is reduced by two thirds, and chickpeas are tender about 6 minutes. Test and season with additional salt and pepper as needed. Remove from the heat and reserve until the fish has finished marinating.

4. Place the remaining 1 tablespoon of olive oil in a small skillet and put it over medium heat. Once the oil shines, add the canned lemon wedges and brown until caramelized, about 3 minutes per side; set aside.

5. Return the skillet with chickpeas over medium heat. Dip the fish into the chickpea mixture and place 3 canned lemon wedges on top of each fillet. Cover and simmer until the fish flakes when cut, about 10 minutes for a 3/4inch thick fillet or 12 minutes for a 1 to 11 / 4inch thick fillet. Sprinkle the remaining tablespoon of coriander over the fish. To serve, place a fillet in a shallow bowl, followed by a large tablespoon of chickpeas.

Nutrition:

- **Calories:** 122 kcal
- **Fat:** 7.1 g
- **Protein:** 6.9 g
- **Cholesterol:** 17 mg
- **Sodium:** 1102 mg

195.   **STUFFED FISH**

Easy/Gluten-free

Preparation Time: 20 minutes

Cooking time: 20 minutes

Servings: 4

Ingredients:

- 2 quarts (8 cups) fish broth
- 1 cup diced yellow onion (about 1 medium onion)
- 1/3 cup diced carrot, large (about 1/2 medium carrot)
- 1/3 cup diced, peeled parsnip (about 1/2 medium parsnip)
- 2 1/2-pounds mix of mild-flavored white skin fish fillets such as cod, halibut, pike, or grouper
- 1/3 cup matzo flour
- 3 large eggs, lightly beaten
- 1 teaspoon finely grated lemon zest (about 1 medium lemon)
- 3 tablespoons of freshly squeezed lemon juice

- 4 teaspoons of kosher salt, plus more as needed
- 1/2 teaspoon freshly ground black pepper, plus more as needed
- Beet horseradish or horseradish mayonnaise with dill, to serve

Directions:

1. Place the fish stock in a large, full pot and simmer over medium heat. Reduce heat to medium-low and keep on low heat.

2. Place the onion, carrot, and parsnip in a food processor equipped with a blade attachment. Process until vegetables are finely chopped, stopping to scrape down sides of the bowl as needed, about 1minute total. Transfer to a large bowl and set aside.

3. Cut the fish into 11/2-inch pieces. Place half in the food processor and process until a ball forms, about 30 seconds. Transfer the ball to the bowl with the vegetables and repeat with the remaining fish.

4. Sprinkle the fish and vegetable mixture with the matzo flour. Add the eggs, lemon zest, lemon juice, and measured salt and pepper. With clean hands, mix until combined (do not squeeze or work too hard). To test the seasoning, form a small patty and place it in the fish stock until firm and well cooked. Try the empanada and add more salt and pepper to the fish mixture as needed. Repeat the seasoning test as necessary.

5. With wet hands and a 1/4 cup measurement, form the fish mixture into 3inchlong ovals. Place on a baking sheet.

6. Gently place the ovals in the simmering broth. Cover with an airtight lid and simmer until firm and well cooked, about 10 minutes. Using a slotted spoon, carefully remove the ovals from the broth and transfer them to a clean baking sheet to cool.

7. Pour the broth through a fine-mesh filter over a sizeable heat resistant container, discarding the solids. Allow the food to cool to room temperature.

8. Meanwhile, place the chilled gefilte fish in a large container with a tightfitting lid and refrigerate. When the broth is cold, pour it into the bowl with the gefilte fish, making sure it is submerged. Cover and refrigerate for at least 1 hour and until overnight.

9. To serve, use a slotted spoon to transfer the gefilte fish from the broth to a serving plate. Serve with beetroot horseradish or dill mayonnaise, if using.

Nutrition:

- **Calories:** 222 kcal
- **Fat:** 7.1 g
- **Protein:** 6.9 g
- **Cholesterol:** 17 mg

196. GRILLED FISH WITH THAI PESTO

Medium/Gluten-free

Preparation Time: 25 minutes

Cooking time: 50 minutes

Servings: 4

Ingredients:

- 3/4 cup well-packed fresh coriander leaves and tender stems
- 1/4 cup well-packed fresh mint leaves
- 3 medium garlic cloves
- 1 medium jalapeño, seeded and coarsely chopped
- 2 tablespoons lemongrass, coarsely chopped
- 2 teaspoons ginger, peeled and chopped
- 2 teaspoons of fish sauce
- 1 medium lime zest
- 1/4 cup plus 1 tablespoon of peanut oil
- 1/2 pound whole sea bass, red snapper or barramundi, gutted and cleaned

Directions:

1. Heat oven to 400 ° F and place a rack in the middle. Combine coriander, mint, garlic, jalapeño, lemongrass, ginger, fish sauce, and lime zest in a food processor and pulse until evenly pureed. With the food processor running, slowly drizzle in 1/4 cup peanut oil and process until the mixture resembles a thick pesto, about 2 minutes.

2. Rinse the fish inside and out and pat dry with paper towels. Season everything with salt and freshly ground black pepper. Spread the herb mixture inside the fish and securely close with a butcher string or toothpicks.

3. Cut a piece of parchment paper or aluminum foil enough to enclose the fish and place it on a baking sheet. Drizzle the foil with the rest of 1 tablespoon of peanut oil. Place the fish on the aluminum foil and fold the aluminum foil (however, do not close too much; leave a little space around the fish). Roast the fish in the oven until the meat is white and firm to the touch, about 40 minutes. Serve immediately.

Nutrition:

- **Calories:** 222 kcal
- **Fat:** 7.1 g
- **Protein:** 6.9 g

- **Cholesterol:** 17 mg
- **Sodium:** 302 mg

---

197.   <u>FISH STEW</u>

Easy/Gluten-free

Preparation Time: 20 minutes

Cooking time: 20 minutes

Servings: 4

Ingredients:

FOR THE BROTH:

- 4 cups of clam juice or fish stock (or the bones of a large, mild-tasting fish plus 4 cups of water)
- 1/2 cup dry white wine
- 1 bay leaf
- 1 sprig of fresh thyme
- 1 fresh sprig of Italian parsley
- 5 whole black peppercorns

FOR THE STEW:

- 1 can (28 ounces) peeled whole tomatoes
- 3 tablespoons olive oil
- 2 medium leeks, cut in half lengthwise and cut into ½-inch pieces (white and light green parts only)
- 1 medium fennel bulb, outer shell discarded, core removed and diced medium
- 2 medium garlic cloves, minced
- Kosher salt
- Freshly ground black pepper
- 1/2 cup dry white wine
- 1 pound small necked clams, scrubbed and soaked in various cold-water changes
- 2 pounds' mild-flavored mixed white fish fillets (such as cod, halibut, or grouper), skinless, cut into 2-inches pieces
- 2 tablespoons coarsely chopped fresh chervil or tarragon leaves
- 2 tablespoons coarsely chopped fresh Italian parsley leaves
- 1 cup aioli (optional)
- Crispy French baguette, to serve

Directions:

For the broth:

1. Place all ingredients in a medium saucepan and bring to a boil over medium-high heat. Reduce heat to low and simmer until flavors melt, about 30 minutes. Strain through a fine-mesh strainer into a medium saucepan and keep warm.

For the stew:

1. Drain the tomatoes and discard the liquid. Using your hands and working in a medium bowl, break the tomatoes into rough ¾-inch pieces, discarding the kernels but keeping the juice and seeds; set aside.

2. Heat the olive oil in a large heavy-bottomed saucepan or a Dutch oven over medium-high heat until it shines. Add the leeks and fennel and cook, occasionally stirring, until the leeks are translucent and the fennel has softened about 5 minutes. Add garlic, season with salt and pepper, and cook until fragrant, about 1 minute more. Add the wine and simmer until it almost evaporates about 3 minutes. Add reserved tomatoes (along with their seeds and juices) and warm broth, stir to combine, and bring to a boil.

3. Reduce the heat to medium-low, add the clams, and simmer until they start to open about 2 to 3 minutes. Meanwhile, season fish lightly with salt and pepper. Gently dip the fish into the broth and simmer, cooking until the fish begins to crumble when you prick it with a fork and the clams open, about 8 to 10 minutes. Test and season with additional salt and pepper as needed. Sprinkle with fresh herbs, scoop into bowls, and (if you choose) top each with a tablespoon of aioli. Serve with the baguette.

Nutrition:

- **Calories:** 222 kcal
- **Fat:** 7.1 g
- **Protein:** 6.9 g
- **Cholesterol:** 12 mg
- **Sodium:** 302 mg

198.   WHOLE ROASTED FISH BASQUAISE

Medium/Gluten-free

Preparation Time: 20 minutes

Cooking time: 50 minutes

Servings: 4

Ingredients:

- 2 Yukon Gold potatoes, cut into small pieces
- 4 tablespoons of olive oil
- 1 onion, thinly sliced

- 1 red bell pepper, seeded, seeded, and cut into thin strips
- 1 green bell pepper, seeded, seeded, and cut into thin strips
- 4 garlic cloves, crushed
- 2 thyme sprigs, leaves only
- 1/2 cup of white wine
- 1 cup chicken broth or light chicken broth
- 1 red snapper, about 2 pounds, scales removed, gills removed, fins trimmed, guts removed, but intact
- Juice of 1 lemon
- 4 sprigs of flat parsley

Directions:

1. Preheat oven to 400 ° F. Place potatoes in a small saucepan and cover with water. Add salt to taste and bring to a boil. Cook for 10 minutes. Vegetables must be firm. Remove them from the water and set aside.

2. On the stove, heat the olive oil in a roasting pan until it almost sizzles. Add the onions and peppers and cook over medium heat until the vegetables are soft and golden. Add garlic and thyme and cook for another 2 to 3 minutes. Add the white wine, scraping the bottom of the pan with a wooden spoon to dislodge all of those good things. Add chicken stock and bring mixture to a boil.

3. Season the fish with salt and freshly ground black pepper inside and out. After the broth and vegetables have been boiling for 5 minutes, put the fish in the pan, add the potatoes, and throw everything in the oven. Cook for about 30 minutes, basting the fish with the juices from the pan 2- or 3-times during cooking.

4. Change the oven setting to roast, remove the pan from the oven, and remove the fish from the broiler pan. Place the fish on a baking sheet and put it under the grill for 35 minutes, or until the skin turns brown and crisp. Watch it: you don't want to burn the thing. Transfer the fish to a serving platter. Add the lemon juice to the pepper and potato mixture, and season with salt and pepper. After a quick blast of heat and a stir or two, pour the mixture over and around the fish. Garnish with parsley and serve immediately.

5. **Note:** Don't neglect the cheeks, the meat on the neck, or the scaly parts between the bones. Feel free to eat with your hands.

6. Now think of all the ways you can improvise on this plate.

Nutrition:

- **Calories:** 213 kcal
- **Fat:** 7.1 g
- **Protein:** 6.9 g

- **Cholesterol:** 17 mg
- **Sodium:** 362 mg

---

199. FISH STUFFED WITH POMEGRANATE SAUCE

Medium/Gluten-free

Preparation Time: 20 minutes

Cooking time: 45 minutes

Servings: 4

Ingredients:

- 1 large or 2pound white fish, about 1/2inch thick: sea bass, halibut, cod, rockfish, or orange
- 1 teaspoon salt
- 1/3 cup olive oil or butter
- 1 onion, peeled and thinly sliced
- 3 garlic cloves, peeled and minced
- 1/4 teaspoon freshly ground black pepper
- 1/4 cup chopped walnuts
- 1 cup of pomegranate juice or 3 tablespoons of pomegranate paste
- 1 tablespoon of candied orange peel
- 2 tablespoons of fresh lime juice
- 1/4 teaspoon ground saffron dissolved in 2 tablespoons hot water
- 1 tablespoon of angelica petals or powder (gold par,) to Decorate
- 2 tablespoons of chopped walnuts, to decorate
- 2 tablespoons of pomegranate seeds, to decorate

Directions:

1. Rinse the fish in cold water. Dry with a paper towel and rub both sides with 1 teaspoon of salt.
2. Heat 1/4 cup oil in a large skillet and brown the onion and garlic. Add all ingredients except saffron water and lime juice and cook for 3 minutes. Mix well and remove from heat.
3. Preheat oven to 400 ° F. Place fish in a baking dish. Fill with the mixture from step 2 and close or sew the cavity. Pour the saffron water, the rest of the oil, and the lime juice over the fish.
4. Place the fish in the oven and bake for 10 to 15 minutes (until the fish flakes easily with a fork), basting occasionally.
5. Arrange the fish in a serving platter. Pour the sauce from the baking dish over the fish. Garnish with angelica petals, walnuts, and pomegranate seeds.

6. Serve with simple steamed rice with saffron.

Nutrition:

- **Calories:** 222 kcal
- **Fat:** 7.1 g
- **Protein:** 6.9 g
- **Cholesterol:** 17 mg
- **Sodium:** 302 mg

---

200.   __KEDGEREE__

Medium/Gluten-free

Preparation Time: 20 minutes

Cooking time: 40 minutes

Servings: 4

Ingredients:

- 1 pound firm skinned white fish fillets, such as turbot, haddock, or cod
- 1 cup milk
- 4 tablespoons of butter
- 5 cups cooked cold white or brown rice
- 1/4 cup chicken or fish broth or water; as necessary
- 1 teaspoon of cayenne pepper
- Salt
- freshly ground black pepper
- 2 eggs
- 2/3 cup heavy cream
- 1 small bunch flatleaf parsley, chopped
- 2 hardboiled eggs, peeled and sliced

Directions:

1. Put the fish in a saucepan with the milk and simmer. Cook the fish until it flakes when you prick it with a fork, and it becomes opaque in the center. The time will depend on the thickness of the fillets. Remove the fish from the pan and discard the milk. Let the fish cool until it can be handled, then remove and discard the skin and break the meat into large scales, removing the errant bones. Set aside.

2. Melt butter in a high-sided skillet over medium heat. Add the rice and stir to coat with the butter. Add the broth and continue to the site, adding more broth if necessary, to prevent the rice from sticking until

it is very hot. Add cayenne and salt and black pepper to taste and stir well. Add the fish, gently turning it with the rice to mix it. Break the eggs into a bowl, add the cream and mix roughly with a fork. Keeping the heat very low, add the egg mixture to the pan and cook very gently, occasionally turning, until the egg is fully cooked, but remains slightly liquid 56 minutes.

3. Remove from heat and serve on hot plates, garnished with parsley and hardboiled eggs.

Nutrition:

- **Calories:** 208 kcal
- **Fat:** 7.1 g
- **Protein:** 6.9 g
- **Cholesterol:** 17 mg
- **Sodium:** 402 mg

Conclusion

A pescatarian is anyone who includes seafood and fish to the vegetarian diet. Different people, for several reasons, may decide to eliminate poultry and meat from their diet but still retain fish. Some vegetarians include fish to their food as they want to not only enjoy the benefits of a plant-based diet but also have a healthy heart. Some others may do this because it suits their taste. While the rest may stick to the pescatarian diet simply because of its impact on the environment.

A pescatarian is someone that includes fish to their diet but avoids meat and other poultry. The term was coined in the early 1990s with a combination of two words, 'Pesce', which means fish and 'vegetarian.' In summary, a pescatarian is anyone who follows the vegetarian diet, but also includes fish and other seafood to his or her diet. The diet is mainly made up of plant-based foods like legumes, healthy fats, nuts, whole grains, and produce with seafood being the major source of protein.

People are normally vegetarian, and we overlook, at our danger, our vegan primate ancestry. One of the world's driving specialists on diet and wellbeing accepts that the closer we approach a thoroughly plant food diet, the more prominent the advantage to our life.

This diet has helped so many people over the years. There is no doubt in my mind that these recipes can assist you in reaching whatever your health and fitness goals are, from weight loss to muscle gain.

People who are just beginning the pescatarian diet may find it difficult to design their meals for the next few weeks. This may cause some people to default eating more of high carb meals, which is not the best way to maintain a healthy balanced diet. One of the great benefits of this diet is that you get to enjoy plenty of omega3 fatty acids from fish, which will lower inflammation in the body.
Hope that you enjoyed the recipes compiled for you here. There are recipes for every taste, budget, and occasion. The recipes are all easy to prepare, and the ingredients and cooking equipment are all readily available at your local grocery store.
Trying out these recipes will make you appreciate the simplicity, variety, and versatility of seafood and a pescetarian diet in general.

Finally, when you buy seafood, you can do the same by buying "sustainable" fish for the marine environment. These fishing methods show that unnecessary damage to marine organisms or not excessive fishing can reduce fish stocks.

And instead of going where you can go, instead of choosing imported fish that travel thousands of miles to reach your destination. You can also help maintain a favorable environmental balance, which in turn encourages fishing, rather than just focusing on the imported ones.

The next step is to…start eating, what else? Pursue a wide variety of foods that you can eat with a pescatarian diet, as well as explore the unique recipes you can create.

Printed in Great Britain
by Amazon